D0932998

ESSENTIAL
EDINBURGH

Original text by Sally Roy
Revised and updated by Robin McKelvie

© AA Media Limited 2010
First published 2008. Revised 2010

ISBN: 978 0 7495-6674-6

Published by AA Publishing, a trading name of AA Media Limited, whose registered office is Fanum House, Basing View, Basingstoke, Hampshire RG21 4EA. Registered number 06112600.

Colour separation: MRM Graphics Ltd
Printed and bound in Italy by Printer Trento S.r.l.

A04192

Enabled by [Ordnance Survey] This product includes mapping data licensed from Ordnance Survey® with the permission of the Controller of Her Majesty's Stationery Office. © Crown copyright 2010. All rights reserved. Licence number 100021153
Transport map © Communicarta Ltd, UK

About this book

Symbols are used to denote the following categories:

✚ map reference to maps on cover

✉ address or location

☎ telephone number

🕐 opening times

✋ admission charge

🍴 restaurant or cafe on premises
or nearby

Ⓜ nearest underground train station

🚍 nearest bus/tram route

🚉 nearest overground train station

⛴ nearest ferry stop

✈ nearest airport

❓ other practical information

ℹ tourist information office

➤ indicates the page where you will
find a fuller description

This book is divided into six sections.

The essence of Edinburgh pages 6–19
Introduction; Features; Food and drink;
Short break

Planning pages 20–33
Before you go; Getting there; Getting
around; Being there

Best places to see pages 34–55
The unmissable highlights of any visit
to Edinburgh

Best things to do pages 56–73
Great lunch venues; stunning views;
places to take the children and more

Exploring pages 74–161
The best places to visit in Edinburgh,
organized by area

Excursions pages 162–181
Places to visit out of town

Maps
All map references are to the maps on
the covers. For example, Arthur's Seat
has the reference ✚ 24K – indicating
the grid square in which it is to be found

Admission prices
£ inexpensive (under £3)
ff moderate (£3–£6)
£££ expensive (over £6)

Hotel prices
Price are per room per night:
£ inexpensive (up to £70)
££ moderate (£70–£150)
£££ expensive (over £150)

Restaurant prices
Price for a three-course meal per person
without drinks or service:
£ inexpensive (up to £20)
££ moderate (£20–£30)
£££ expensive (over £30)

Contents

The essence of...

Edinburgh is the capital of Scotland, with everything a capital should have – a sense of history, superb architecture, great museums and a vibrant cultural life. Its townscape rates among the finest in Europe, the streets and squares punctuated by spires and cupolas and dotted with leafy spaces. Its compact middle is ringed with village-like suburbs that retain their sense of identity, while the proximity of hills and sea adds to the city's beauty. With its face set confidently to the future as Scotland's longed-for autonomy has become a fact, Edinburgh is experiencing a new sense of purpose, making this a perfect time to enjoy one of Europe's most vibrant and visually stunning cities.

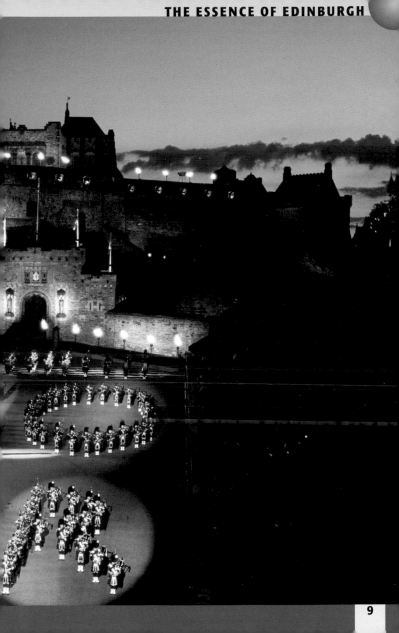

features

It's hard to view Edinburgh dispassionately; no one could be lukewarm about a city with so much history, character, charm and beauty. "Fur coat and nae knickers" say the city's detractors, but there's little wrong with keeping up appearances and presenting one's best face to the world. And what a face. From the cobblestones of the Royal Mile, lined with ancient tenements, to the cool restrained splendour of the New Town terraces, there's always something to delight the eye. The big set pieces – the castle, Holyrood, medieval and classical Edinburgh – never disappoint, but there's so much else beside. The hidden wynds (narrow lanes) and closes of the Old Town, the quiet streets and tucked-away mews in the New, the villas in the tree-lined avenues of Morningside are all just as much essential elements in the townscape as is the brooding presence of Arthur's Seat. Even the bleak outer housing developments and the squalor behind the glories are part of the package, ingredients that balance what might otherwise be bland perfection.

Take time to enjoy it all: a marvellous city whose attractions are set against a glorious backdrop, and whose people are among the kindest and couthiest (friendliest) you could hope to meet.

GEOGRAPHY
● Edinburgh lies south of the Firth of Forth on Scotland's east coast.
● The city's highest point is Arthur's Seat, 251m (823ft), while the seaport of Leith and the waterside areas of Newhaven, Portobello and Cramond lie at sea level.

● The Water of Leith runs northeast, passing through Edinburgh and reaching the Firth of Forth at Leith.

CLIMATE

Edinburgh's climate is typical of the northeastern coast; fairly dry and windy, with lowish average temperatures. Although drier than Scotland's west coast, it can rain at any time. Winter will usually bring frosts and snow. In summer, east coast sea-mists, known as "haar", can affect the city.

THE CITY

This is a compact city: Edinburgh's population lives within the boundary of the Firth of Forth to the north and the southern bypass. Within the city there are 30 designated conservation areas and more than 3,000 listed buildings.

ECONOMY

Edinburgh is the second-largest financial and administrative base in Britain and the majority of employment here is provided by service activities; insurance and banking are the prime sectors. Large numbers are employed in healthcare, local government, and, since devolution in 1999, in Scottish national government. Tourism is also of economic importance.

food & drink

Scottish cuisine revels in fine local ingredients including wild salmon, beef and soft fruit such as raspberries; cakes and puddings are a speciality, and don't forget to sample some buttery shortbread and sweet Edinburgh Rock.

WHAT TO EAT IN EDINBURGH
No matter what you'd like to eat you'll probably find it in cosmopolitan Edinburgh, but seek out Scottish specialities, many of which you won't find south of the border.

SCOTTISH INGREDIENTS
Scotland has some of the best raw ingredients in the world, with land, river and sea contributing superb produce. Aberdeen

Angus beef is renowned, game such as venison, grouse and pheasant is plentiful in season, and there's an abundance of the freshest of fish, including salmon, and shellfish, while Scotland's soft fruits have an intensity of flavour.

With such ingredients to hand, it seems ironic that the Scots' diet was once among Europe's unhealthiest, with many inhabitants revelling in oversalted and oversweetened dishes, and some Scots men proudly boasting they never ate vegetables. But things have changed radically in recent years and there's a renewed pride in fresh local produce and also in traditional recipes.

EATING THROUGH THE DAY

Traditionally breakfast meant porridge, the classic hot oatmeal dish, properly eaten with salt, but nicer with milk and sugar. Cured kippers (smoked herrings) are another favourite, or black or fruit pudding to accompany the egg and bacon. Oatcakes, soft bread "morning rolls" and marmalade itself are all Scots originals.

Lunch is the time for something light: a smoked-salmon sandwich, prawn salad or a bowl of good Scots

soup. Scotch broth is famous, but try cock-a-leekie, made with chicken, leeks and prunes, or cullen skink, a delicate fish and potato broth. Bridies, a pastry turnover stuffed with meat and onion, mutton pies, made with crisp hot-water pastry, and stovies, potato and onion, are traditional lunchtime favourites.

Tea and baking are taken very seriously in Edinburgh, and you'll find excellent teashops and bakers churning out delectable cakes and biscuits. Shortbread should be high on the list: the sweet-toothed will love "millionaire's shortbread" with its layers of soft toffee and chocolate.

Dinner brings steaks, game and fish, plainly cooked or as the base for more sophisticated dishes. Haggis, the famous oatmeal, offal and onion dish traditionally simmered in a sheep's stomach, is delicious when properly made.

Puddings are awesomely sweet; favourites include clootie dumpling, a fruit pudding boiled in a cloth, Scots trifle, rich in sherry, jam and cream, or cranachan, made from toasted oatmeal folded into whipped cream and served with berries.

FROM WHISKY TO IRN-BRU

Tea is the liquid mainstay, with coffee gaining in popularity. Some Edinburgh folk love fizzy sweet drinks, a favourite being Irn-Bru, famously advertised as "brewed in Scotland from girders". Scots beer differs from English; heavy is the nearest equivalent to English bitter and beers are graded by the shilling, a system indicating the potency – the higher the shilling, the

stronger the beer. Look for beers from Edinburgh's small local breweries, or try export or lager.

Whole volumes have been written about whisky. The choice lies between blended, a careful mix of grain and malt, and single malt – with literally hundreds to choose from. Try a few, find one you like and drink it neat or with water, the best way to appreciate the subtle taste.

Short break

If you have only a limited period to enjoy Edinburgh, to ensure you take away some unforgettable memories make time for a few of these:

● **Take an open-air bus** (➤ 138) ride around the city's main sights to get your bearings.

● **Spend a leisurely morning** walking down the Royal Mile (➤ 52–53), making sure you explore its evocative wynds (lanes) and closes to get a real sense of Edinburgh's history.

● **Head away from the heart of the city** to hunt for presents and souvenirs in the enticing small shops in areas such as Stockbridge (➤ 152), William Street, the Grassmarket (➤ 84) and Victoria Street (➤ 92–93).

- **Seek out** one of Edinburgh's many vantage points to enjoy the panorama of the city's superb setting – climb Arthur's Seat (► 36–37), stand on the castle ramparts (► 38–39) or walk up Calton Hill (► 114) for some of the best views.

- **Track down local entertainment;** in summer choose from Festival events or the Tattoo. In winter there's everything from Celtic rock to Scottish pantomime and Hogmanay (► 25).

- **Join the Saturday afternoon crowds** in Princes Street (► 121) to get a feel for Edinburgh's people, then head for one of the smart cafe-bars on George Street (► 117).

● **Climb the Scott Monument** for views up and down Princes Street and across to the Mound and Edinburgh Castle (➤ 54–55).

● **Sample some Scottish food and drink;** specialities range from shortbread and haggis to Edinburgh Rock (candy) and malt whisky, and you're bound to find something to enjoy.

● **Take a couple of hours** to stroll around the Georgian splendour of New Town, one of Europe's finest and most elegant examples of 18th-century town planning (➤ 44–45).

● **Relax in Princes Street Gardens,** where you can have lunch, catch a band concert, admire the castle's silhouette and set your watch by the Floral Clock (➤ 122).

Planning

EDINBU
INSPIRING CAPIT

Before you go

WHEN TO GO

JAN	FEB	MAR	APR	MAY	JUN	JUL	AUG	SEP	OCT	NOV	DEC
4°C	4°C	6°C	9°C	12°C	16°C	17°C	16°C	15°C	12°C	7°C	5°C
39°F	39°F	43°F	48°F	54°F	61°F	63°F	61°F	59°F	54°F	45°F	41°F

 High season   Low season

Edinburgh experiences defined seasons. Spring (March to May) has a mixture of sunshine and showers although winter conditions can continue into March. May and early June are often the finest months with long clear sunny days but some chilly nights. June has long daylight hours but the end of the month is the start of the busy school holidays. The later summer months are less predictable with a fair chance of rain or thunderstorms. September is the official start of autumn but the season really starts in October when the colder days set in. Winter (December to February) can be cold, dreary and dark with the occasional bright frosty day to lighten the mood. Snow is a possibility but does not usually settle long in the city.

WHAT YOU NEED

● Required
○ Suggested
▲ Not required

Some countries require a passport to remain valid for a minimum period (usually at least six months) beyond the date of entry – check before you travel.

	UK	Germany	USA	Netherlands	Spain
Passport	▲	●	●	●	●
Visa (Regulations can change – check before booking your journey)	▲	▲	▲	▲	▲
Onward or Return Ticket	▲	○	○	○	○
Health Inoculations	▲	▲	▲	▲	▲
Health Documentation (► 23, Health Insurance)	▲	●	●	●	●
Travel Insurance	○	○	○	○	○
Driving Licence (national)	●	●	●	●	●
Car Insurance Certificate (if own car)	▲	●	●	●	●
Car Registration Document (if own car)	▲	●	●	●	●

WEBSITES

- www.edinburgh.org
VisitScotland's dedicated website for Edinburgh and the Lothians
- www.visitscotland.com
Scotland's national tourism site
- www.edinburghguide.com
General information
- www.cac.org.uk
City of Edinburgh museums and galleries

TOURIST OFFICES AT HOME

In the UK

Scottish Booking and Info Centre
VisitScotland
Fairways Business Park
Deer Park Avenue, Livingston
Edinburgh EH54 8AF
☎ 0845 225 5121
www.edinburgh.org
info@visitscotland.com

In the USA

VisitBritain
551 Fifth Avenue, Suite 701
New York
NY 10176
☎ 1 800 462 2748
www.visitbritain.us
travelinfo@visitbritain.com

HEALTH INSURANCE

The National Health Service (NHS) provides free treatment for all EU nationals and residents of countries with which the UK has a reciprocal agreement – bring your European Health Insurance Card (EHIC) from your home country.

Visitors from countries outside the EU should obtain comprehensive travel insurance before leaving.

TIME DIFFERENCES

GMT	Edinburgh	Germany	USA (NY)	Netherlands	Spain
12 noon	12 noon	1PM	7AM	1PM	1PM

Like those in the rest of the UK, Scottish clocks go forward by one hour on the last weekend in March to give British Summer Time (BST). Clocks go back to rejoin Greenwich Mean Time (GMT) the last weekend in October.

NATIONAL HOLIDAYS

Scottish public holidays may vary from place to place and their dates from year to year; thus, although Edinburgh may be on holiday at certain times, other Scottish towns and cities will not necessarily be having a public holiday.

1 Jan *New Year's Day
2 Jan *Holiday
Mar/Apr *Good Friday, Easter Monday
First Mon May *May Day Bank Holiday
Mon, mid- to late May Victoria Holiday

Last Mon in Aug August Bank Holiday
3rd Mon in Sep Autumn Holiday
25 Dec *Christmas Day
26 Dec *Boxing Day

* throughout Scotland

WHAT'S ON WHEN

January Burns Night: Edinburgh celebrates the birthday of Scotland's national poet on 25 January, with traditional haggis dinners and draughts of whisky in hotels and restaurants all over the city.

April Edinburgh Science Festival: Lectures and events covering all branches of science and technology, held in over 40 venues city-wide.

May Scottish International Children's Festival: The largest festival of performing arts in the UK for children and young people.

June Edinburgh International Film Festival: The world's longest-running film festival has both mainstream and independent new releases, with interviews, discussions and debate (Filmhouse, 88 Lothian Road, Edinburgh EH3 9BZ, tel: 0131 228 4051; www.edfilmfest.org.uk). Royal Highland Show: Highlight of Scotland's country year, with a huge variety of events over five days, including pedigree livestock judging, show-jumping and agricultural displays.

August Edinburgh International Festival: Three weeks of top-quality opera, dance, music and theatre from all around the world, at a variety of locations throughout the city. It's advisable to book tickets as far ahead as possible (The Hub, Castlehill, Royal Mile, Edinburgh EH1 2NE, tel: 0131 473 2000 for reservations; 0131 473 2099 for general information; www.eif.co.uk).

Edinburgh Festival Fringe: The world's largest arts festival, held over three weeks, with exhibitions, music, dance, comedy and shows for children (The Fringe Office, 180 High Street, Royal Mile, Edinburgh EH1 1QS, tel: 0131 226 0026; www.edfringe.com).

Edinburgh Military Tattoo: A spectacular display of music, entertainment and theatre with a military theme, set against the stunning backdrop of Edinburgh Castle. It's a very popular event, so book your tickets as early as possible (Castle Esplanade, Edinburgh Castle, Tattoo Office: 32 Market Street, Edinburgh EH1 1QB, tel: 0131 225 1188; www.edinburgh-tattoo.co.uk).

Edinburgh Book Festival: An annual event since 1998, the festival occupies a tented village in Charlotte Square, and attracts a wide spectrum of authors for talks, readings and book signing sessions. Many events are specifically geared towards children (Charlotte Square Gardens, Edinburgh EH2 4DR, tel: 0845 373 5888 for box office; www.edbookfest.co.uk).

Jazz and Blues Festival: The complete gamut of jazz forms can be found in the many venues that host this international 10-day festival, with musicians from all over the world (89 Giles Street, Edinburgh EH6 6BZ, tel: 0131 467 5200; www.edinburghjazzfestival.co.uk).

September *Firework Concert:* A fantastic firework display against the backdrop of the Castle, accompanied by classical music. The fireworks are visible from a variety of locations throughout the city, such as Calton Hill. www.eif.co.uk/fireworks

Doors Open Day: Some of the finest private houses in Edinburgh are opened to members of the public on one day of the year; contact the Cockburn Association, Trunk's Close, 55 High Street EH1 1SR, tel: 0131 557 8686; www.cockburnassociation.org.uk.

Edinburgh Mela: Scotland's biggest intercultural festival with colourful celebrations of music and dance, plus arts and crafts, and street performers; www.edinburgh-mela.co.uk.

December/January *Edinburgh Hogmanay:* This spectacular street party, centred on Princes Street, has become Europe's biggest winter festival, with street theatre, ceilidhs and general merrymaking. www.edinburghshogmanay.org

Getting there

BY AIR

Edinburgh Airport

9.6km (6 miles) to city centre

🚌 N/A

🚆 30 minutes

🚗 20–30 minutes

Britain's national airline, British Airways (tel: 0844 493 0787; www.ba.com), operates frequent scheduled flights in and out of Edinburgh; the airport is also served by BMI, Air France, Aer Lingus, KLM, Lufthansa, Ryanair and easyJet. Intercontinental flights arriving in Britain normally route via London, though limited transatlantic direct flights are available.

FROM EDINBURGH AIRPORT

Coaches Airlink coach service to central Edinburgh runs every 10 minutes on weekdays and less often at evenings and weekends. It costs £6 return, £3.50 one-way and takes about 30 minutes. Buy tickets from the tourist information office inside the airport, the ticket booth or on the bus. A route map is available from the information desk and is shown inside the bus. The route brings you in past the zoo and Murrayfield stadium, and along Princes Street to Waverley Bridge and the rail station. Buses, including all public buses, leave from the arrivals area in front of the terminal building.

Taxis Taxis wait outside the arrivals hall in the rank beside the coach park. The journey takes about 25 minutes and costs around £17. Edinburgh Airport Taxis (tel: 0131 344 3344).

Car Rental International rental firms such as Avis, Hertz and Budget have offices at Edinburgh Airport (tel: 0844 481 8989).

ARRIVING BY RAIL

Edinburgh has two major rail stations: Edinburgh Haymarket and Edinburgh Waverley. Waverley is the central station for onward travel within Scotland. Internal services are run by First ScotRail (tel: 08457 55

00 33; www.firstscotrail.com). For details of fares and services on Britain's National Rail network contact the National Rail Enquiry Service (tel: 08457 484950; www.nationalrail.co.uk).

ARRIVING BY COACH

Coaches arrive from England, Wales and Scotland at the St Andrews Street bus station in Edinburgh. The main coach companies operating to and from the bus station are National Express (tel: 08705 808080; www.nationalexpress.com) and Scottish Citylink (tel: 08705 505050; www.citylink.co.uk). Other Scottish bus companies also operate into the terminal, which has an information office.

ARRIVING BY CAR

Driving in the city is difficult with its one-way systems, narrow streets, Red Routes (double and single red lines indicate that stopping to park, board or alight from a vehicle is prohibited) and dedicated bus routes. Limited on-street parking is mostly pay-and-display (from 8:30am to 6:30pm Monday–Saturday). There are designated parking areas, to the south of Princes Street; the biggest is at Greenside Place, off Leith Street.

Getting around

PUBLIC TRANSPORT

Internal Flights operate to Inverness, Kirkwall, Stornoway, Sumburgh, and Wick, also to Birmingham, Bristol, Cardiff, Exeter, Jersey, Lerwick, Leeds Bradford, London City, London Heathrow, London Gatwick, London Stansted, Manchester, Norwich and Southampton.

Trains Edinburgh has two mainline railway stations: Edinburgh Waverley and Edinburgh Haymarket. Most internal rail services are run by First ScotRail (tel: 08457 55 00 33; www.firstscotrail.com). For details of fares and services call the National Rail Enquiry Scheme (tel: 08457 484950; www.nationalrail.co.uk) or visit the information desk at Waverley Station.

Buses The chief Edinburgh operator is Lothian Buses (for information tel: 0131 555 6363; www.lothianbuses.co.uk). Lothian Buses has three travel shops (27 Hanover Street, Shandwick Place and Waverley Bridge, Princes Street).

Trams At the time of publication a new public tram system for the city is under construction, with a line connecting Leith to the city centre and beyond to the airport. It is due to be completed some time between 2011 and 2013.

Boat Trips The *Maid of the Forth* leaves daily from Hawes Pier, South Queensferry, sailing beneath the Forth Rail Bridge to Inchcolm Island, where you can take the option to disembark. Easter and October (tel: 0131 331 5000; www.maidoftheforth.co.uk). From North Berwick, the *Sula II* sails two to four times daily around the Bass Rock. Easter and September (tel: 01620 892838; www.sulaboattrips.co.uk).

TAXIS
City centre taxis are black and can be hailed on the street, picked up at ranks or you can call Central Taxis (tel: 0131 229 2468) or City Cabs (tel: 0131 228 1211).

FARES AND TICKETS
Buses You need to pay on board and ensure you have the exact fare as no change is given. Put the money into the slot in front of the driver and take your ticket from the machine behind the driver. Standard adult fare for a single journey is £1.20. A flat-rate single journey at night (any distance) is

£3. A CitySingle costing £24 for 20 trips is available from Lothian travel shops (▶ 27). A child aged 5–15 pays 70p to travel any distance. You can buy a Dayticket from the driver for a day's unlimited travel (adult £3, child £2.40). Timetables and tickets are available at the Travel Shops. An enlarged map and timetable on the bridge outside Waverley Station has additional information about the night bus service into the suburbs.

✓**Edinburgh Pass** This card gives free access to more than 30 attractions in Edinburgh and the Lothians. It includes free bus travel, including airport bus transfer, and special offers from some shops, restaurants and Festival events. A free guidebook explains what's on offer. Cost: 1-day pass £24, 2-day £36 and 3-day £48. You can buy online at www.edinburgh.org/pass or from the Tourist Information Centres at the airport or in the city.

DRIVING
- Speed limit on motorways: 110kph (70mph).
- Speed limit on main roads: 100kph (60mph).
- Speed limit on minor roads: 50–65kph (30–40mph) advisable, and compulsory in built-up areas.
- Seatbelts must be worn in front and back seats at all times
- Random breath testing. Never drive under the influence of alcohol.
- Non-leaded, leaded and diesel fuel is available from all service stations. This normally comes in three grades, premium unleaded, 4-star and city diesel. Petrol stations are normally open 6am–10pm Monday–Saturday and 8am–8pm on Sundays, though some (often self-service) are open 24 hours. All take credit and direct debit cards and many have well-stocked shops.
- If you break down driving your own car call the AA and join on the spot if you are not already a member (tel: 0800 887766; www.theAA.com). If you are driving a rental car, call the emergency number supplied by the rental company; most rental firms provide a rescue service.

CAR RENTAL
Local firms include:
Arnold Clark (tel: 0131 458 1501)
Edinburgh Self Drive (tel: 0131 229 8686)
Condor Self Drive (tel: 0131 229 6333).

Being there

TOURIST OFFICES

**Edinburgh and Scotland
Info Centre**
Princes Mall
3 Princes Street
EH12 2QP
☎ 0845 225 5121
www.edinburgh.org
www.visitscotland.com

**Edinburgh Airport Tourist
Info Desk**
Ingliston
EH12 9DN

MONEY

Scotland's currency is pounds sterling (£) issued by the three major Scottish banks (the Bank of Scotland, the Royal Bank of Scotland and the Clydesdale Bank) in notes of £1, £5, £10, £20, £50 and £100 (the latter is rarely found and there is no English equivalent). Scottish notes are legal tender throughout the UK, and Bank of England notes are legal tender in Scotland. All coins are issued by the Royal Mint, with no separate Scottish coins; there are 1p, 2p, 5p, 10p, 20p, 50p, £1 and £2 coins. Note that Bank of Scotland, Royal Bank of Scotland and Clydesdale Bank ATMs issue only their own respective notes.

You can exchange foreign currency and travellers' cheques at banks and bureaux de change.

TIPS/GRATUITIES

Yes ✓   No ✗

Restaurants (service not included)	✓	10–15%
Cafés/Bars (if table service)	✓	change
Tour guides	✓	£1–£2
Taxis	✓	10%
Porters (depending on amount of luggage)	✓	£1–£3
Chambermaids	✓	change
Hairdressers	✓	10%
Cloakroom attendants	✓	change
Toilets	✓	change

POSTAL AND INTERNET SERVICES

Post offices are open 9–5:30 Monday–Friday and 9am–12:30pm Saturday; Edinburgh's main post office at the St James Centre is also open until 5:30pm on Saturday. For Royal Mail queries: Customer Services (tel: 0845 722 3344). You can buy stamps in gift shops, stores and supermarkets.

Many hotels have internet access available for guests and main public libraries also have internet access. For internet cafes in Edinburgh try easyInternetcafé, 58 Rose Street, EH2 2YQ (tel: 0131 220 3577, 7:30am–10pm, £1 per 30 minutes) or Moviebank, 53 London Street, EH3 6LX (tel: 0131 557 1011, Mon–Sat 2–10, Sun 2–9, 3p per minute).

TELEPHONES

Calls can be made using credit cards, phone company credit cards, phone cards (available in units of £2, £5 and £10) and coins. Edinburgh code: 0131; operator: 100; directory enquiries: 118500.

International dialling codes

From Edinburgh to:
Germany: 00 49
USA and Canada: 00 1
Netherlands: 00 31

Emergency number

Police, fire, ambulance: 999

EMBASSIES AND CONSULATES

USA ☎ 09068 200290

Netherlands ☎ 0131 524 9436

Germany ☎ 0131 337 2323

Spain ☎ 0131 220 1843

HEALTH ADVICE

Health Services Accident and emergency treatment is free to everyone. The 24-hour casualty department is at the Royal Infirmary of Edinburgh, 51 Little France, Old Dalkeith Road, Edinburgh EH16 4SA (tel: 0131 536 1000). **Dental Services** Dental services are free only to UK citizens who fall into certain categories. For emergencies, there is a free walk-in dental clinic in Edinburgh: the Chalmers Dental Centre, Level 7, Lauriston Building, 1 Lauriston Place (tel: 0131 536 4800).
Drugs Prescription and non-prescription drugs and medicine are available from chemists (pharmacies), which are often distinguished by a green

cross. Some supermarkets have a pharmacy shop within the store. A pharmacist will be able to advise on the treatment of simple complaints.
Sun Advice Some summers can be hot – use sun screen or cover up.
Safe Water Tap water is safe to drink; bottled water is widely available.

PERSONAL SAFETY

Policemen wear a peaked flat hat with a black-and-white chequered band; they are friendly and approachable and will give directions and information willingly. In most tourist areas the main danger is petty theft.

- Do not carry more cash than you need.
- Beware of pickpockets, particularly in the main tourist areas.
- Areas to avoid at night include backstreet and dockside areas of Leith, wynds (narrow lanes) leading off Royal Mile, the footpaths across The Meadows and some peripheral housing schemes.

Police assistance ☎ 999 from any call box for true emergencies only.

ELECTRICITY

The power supply in Edinburgh is 240 volts AC. Sockets accept three-pin plugs. North American visitors will need a transformer and adaptor for electrical appliances, European and Australasian visitors an adaptor only.

OPENING HOURS

In addition, most shops in central Edinburgh are open until 8pm on Thursday and many open 12–5 on Sunday. Tourist-oriented shops are also open on Sunday all over the city. Some city-centre banks remain open until 5 or 5:30. Edinburgh has all-day licensing in its pubs and bars, which are normally open 11am–11pm or later, with nightclubs going on much later.

LANGUAGE

You'll have no difficulty in understanding the people of Edinburgh, who tend automatically to modulate their accent when speaking to non-Scots. However, there are many words and expressions that are uniquely Scots and used in everyday conversation, here are a few:

auld old; Edinburgh is often called Auld Reekie, a reference to its smoking chimney-pots which once cast a pall over the city

awfy very; a person might be described as "awfy auld"

belong come from; an Edinburgh native says "I belong tae Edinburgh"

ben mountain; Ben Nevis is the highest in Scotland and the UK

blether to chatter or a garrulous person; "she's an awfy blether"

bonnie pretty, attractive; "that's a bonnie blink" meaning an attractive view

brae slope or hillside

braw fine, "he's a braw laddie"

burn stream

cairn a pile of stones, often on the top of a hill or acting as a memorial

ceilidh an informal gathering to tell stories and sing songs; now often an organized entertainment with a Scottish theme

clan Highland tribe or family group owing allegiance to a chief

couthy homey and comfortable

douce gentle and kind; can be used to describe weather conditions

dram a drink of whisky

dreich dreary, wet and dull; used about the weather but also about people and gatherings

first-foot the first visit paid to neighbours and friends after the start of New Year, traditionally with a bottle of whisky

fouter fiddle around

glen a Highland valley

gloaming dusk

guttered drunk

haar fine summer sea mist found on the east coast

harling mixture of limestone and gravel used to cover exterior house walls

hen affectionate and informal mode of address to a female

Hogmanay New Year's Eve

ken to know; either a fact or a person "D'ye ken the High Street?", "I dinnae ken Jock Fisher"

kirk church

laird estate landowner

lassie girl

lugs ears

lum chimney; as in "lang may your lum reek" — ie good health

manse vicarage; the home of the minister

messages food shopping; "I'm awa' tae get the messages"

policies grounds or parkland surrounding a substantial house

pend vaulted passage or archway

quaich a two-handled drinking bowl

sarnie sandwich

Sassenach originally a non-Gaelic speaking Lowlander, now usually a non-Scot

scunnered displeased, fed up

stay live; "I stay in Edinburgh"

stravaig wander aimlessly, and pleasurably, about

stushie argument, fight

trews tartan trousers

wynd narrow lane between houses

Best places to see

1 Arthur's Seat

Edinburgh is unique in Europe in possessing a craggy peak within a stone's throw of the heart of the city, the perfect antidote to crowds and culture.

Holyrood Park (➤ 103) and Edinburgh itself are dominated by Arthur's Seat, the extinct volcano soaring 251m (823ft) above the city. The volcano erupted 325 million years ago during the early

Carboniferous era; its other remnants make up the Castle Rock and Calton Hill (➤ 114). Geologists can trace the stages of today's rock formations – the summit marks where the cone erupted, while molten rocks formed the sills such as Salisbury Crags and Samson's Ribs. Erosion during the Ice Age laid bare the inside of the volcano, isolating the twin peaks of Arthur's Seat and the Crow Hill.

Explanations for the name vary; some believe it to be a corruption of the Gaelic name for "archers", others claim the Normans associated it with King Arthur.

You can climb Arthur's Seat from a path starting near St Margaret's Well just inside the Palace of Holyroodhouse entrance to the park; the path divides at the start of Hunter's Bog valley and either branch leads to the summit. Take the right-hand one to go along the path called the Radical Road, which runs directly beneath the rockface of Salisbury Crags, or the left, through the Dasses, to the top. Easiest of all is to drive to the parking area near Dunsapie Loch; from here it's a short, steep climb to the top, with one or two rocky scrambles to give you a feeling of real achievement. However you get there, it's worth it for the panorama of the city, the Firth of Forth, the Pentland Hills and the coastline to the east of Edinburgh.

✚ 24K ✉ Holyrood Park ☎ 0131 652 8150 (Historic Scotland Ranger Service) 🕐 Open access 🖐 Free 🚌 35 to palace entrance, other buses to perimeter ❓ No vehicular access, except to Dunsapie Loch on Sun

2 Edinburgh Castle

www.historic-scotland.gov.uk

Redolent with 1,000 years of history, the courtyards and buildings of Edinburgh's main tourist attraction live up to its dominant position.

Edinburgh Castle rises from an extinct volcanic outcrop at the top of the Royal Mile. From the Esplanade, used in August for the Military Tattoo, the 19th-century gatehouse gives access to the heart of the castle complex. In the 12th century St Margaret's Chapel was built by David I in memory of his mother, on the highest point of the Castle Rock. Around and below the chapel are the defensive batteries, and buildings such as the 1742 Governor's House, still used as the Governor's official residence, the Great Hall with its hammerbeam roof, and the Palace Block, a royal palace from the time of James I. Here, in 1566, Mary, Queen of Scots gave birth to James VI, who became James I of England. The Scottish Crown Jewels are the focal point of an exhibition telling

their story and that of the Stone of Destiny, returned to Scotland from Westminster Abbey where it had lain since 1296.

Explore the vaults known as the French Prisons below the Great

Hall; the name recalls their use in the Napoleonic Wars. Here, too, is the Prisons of War exhibition. On the ramparts is the siege gun known as Mons Meg, which was given to James II in 1457 and could fire a 267kg (608lb) stone nearly 3km (1.8 miles). Today, the only gun fired regularly from the castle is the daily 1 o'clock gun, echoing from the Mills Mount Battery.

✚ 13H ✉ Edinburgh Castle, Castle Hill
☎ 0131 225 9846 🕐 Apr–Sep 9:30–6;
Oct–Mar 9:30–5. Last ticket 45 mins
before closing. Closed 25, 26 Dec;
check for New Year 💵 Expensive
🍴 Restaurant and cafe (£–££)
🚌 23, 27, 41, 42

3 National Museum of Scotland

www.nms.ac.uk

An eye-catching modern building houses more than 10,000 objects telling the story of Scotland's history, people, culture and achievements.

The National Museum of Scotland opened in 1998 as an extension of the old Royal Museum, itself a collection of natural history and decorative arts housed in a Victorian building embellished with splendid cast-iron work, that is currently being refurbished and will fully re-open in 2011. A new national museum for Scotland had been mooted since the early 1950s, and the finished complex provides the perfect foil for the superb collections within.

The museum is divided into seven main sections, each concentrating on a theme in the development of Scotland, and illustrating this through exhibits, display boards, and interactive information. From the geological formation of the landscape move on to wildlife, historical and modern land use and a section on early people, where a group of sculptures by Eduardo Paolozzi (b.1924) is decked with ancient jewellery and objects. The next level looks at the

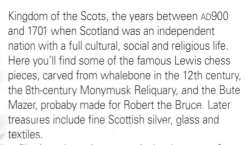

Kingdom of the Scots, the years between AD900 and 1701 when Scotland was an independent nation with a full cultural, social and religious life. Here you'll find some of the famous Lewis chess pieces, carved from whalebone in the 12th century, the 8th-century Monymusk Reliquary, and the Bute Mazer, probaby made for Robert the Bruce. Later treasures include fine Scottish silver, glass and textiles.

Displays show the country's development after the Union with England until the Industrial Revolution, highlighting the industries that made 19th-century Scotland the workshop of the world. The final level is devoted to sporting Scotland and a Scottish Sports Hall of Fame. The roof terrace gives fine views over the city.

🚩 17J 🖂 Chambers Street ☎ 0131 247 4422 🕔 Daily 10 5. Closed 25 Dec 🎟 Free 🍴 Tower Restaurant (£££; ► 96), also two cafes (£–££) 🚌 2, 23, 27, 35, 41, 42 ❓ Regular lunchtime lectures; guided general and themed tours; free portable sound guide

4 National Gallery of Scotland

www.nationalgalleries.org

Superb Old Master and Scottish paintings, displayed in sumptuously decorated galleries, make the National Gallery a draw for all visitors.

Perhaps the greatest attraction of the National Gallery of Scotland is its size, for this comprehensive and high-quality collection can be enjoyed in a leisurely hour or two. Housed in a splendid Classical Revival building designed by William Playfair in 1848, it spans the history of European painting from the Italian Renaissance to French Impressionism. The National Gallery complex also includes the Royal Scottish Academy Building (RSA), which is one of Europe's premier venues for international exhibitions. The two buildings are connected via the Weston Link, which offers further cultural opportunities, as well as shops, a cafe and a restaurant.

Italian Renaissance pictures include a lovely *Madonna and Child* by Verrocchio and Raphael's *Bridgwater Madonna*, part of the Duke of Sutherland's collection.

The loan of this painting in 1946 helped the National Gallery to gain international significance. Northern Renaissance pictures include Hugo van der Goes' Trinity altarpiece, commissioned in the 15th century for an Edinburgh church. Italy is represented by Titian and Tintoretto and Spain by El Greco and Velazquez – look for the superb and tactile picture entitled *An Old Woman Cooking Eggs*, where you can practically feel the eggshell. Works by French artists include Nicolas Poussin's cerebral and detached cycle of *The Seven Sacraments* (c1640), and some superb Impressionist pictures glowing with light.

Leave time to enjoy the Scottish collection, housed in an underground extension, built in the 1970s. This concentrates mainly on 18th- and 19th-century artists such as Allan Ramsay, Henry Raeburn and David Wilkie; Raeburn's engaging portrait, *The Reverend Robert Walker Skating*, is among the gallery's most popular pictures.

✚ 5D ✉ The Mound ☎ 0131 624 6200; recorded info 0131 332 2266 🕐 Fri–Wed 10–5, Thu 10–7. Closed 25–26 Dec ✋ Free 🍴 Cafe, restaurant (£–££) 🚌 3, 10, 17, 23, 27, 44. Free bus links with all five national galleries ❓ Lectures and changing exhibitions

5 New Town

**One of Europe's greatest examples of
Georgian town planning, New Town
combines crescents, squares and circuses
into a harmonious whole.**

By the mid-18th century the crowded tenements and narrow streets of old Edinburgh were no longer adequate to house the population and institutions of the burgeoning city. A competition was launched with a view to building a fine "New Town" to the north; the winning design was by James Craig and construction began in 1767. The Nor' Loch, on the site of Princes Street Gardens (➤ 122) was drained, and the North Bridge built to link the Old Town with the new. The first stage comprised three parallel streets, George, Queen and Princes (➤ 121), linking St Andrew Square (➤ 126) and Charlotte Square (➤ 116), the triumphant facades of the latter designed by Robert Adam in 1791. The more prosperous citizens flocked to live here necessitating further development. Robert Reid, William Playfair and James Gillespie Graham laid out the magnificent streets around Great King Street, the Royal Circus and Moray Place, a highly successful amalgam of interlinking crescents, octagons and ovals. This was followed between 1817 and 1860 by the construction of the West End, with Melville Crescent at its heart.

The result is the world's largest Georgian city development, with more than 11,000 listed properties. Happily, despite the appalling redevelopment of Princes Street in the 1960s, most has remained untouched. More than three-quarters of New Town houses are still in residential use, making the entire area an unchanged enclave.

➕ 4D ✉ New Town ✋ Free 🍴 Restaurants, bars, pubs and cafes throughout the area (£–£££; ➤ 130–135)
🚌 13, 19, 23, 27, 29, 37, 41, 42

6 Our Dynamic Earth

www.dynamicearth.co.uk

Edinburgh's Millennium Landmark project has brought a state-of-the-art attraction to Holyrood, the heart of devolved Scotland.

Against the backdrop of Salisbury Crags rises a light and airy structure, with a translucent spiked and tented roof, fronted by a sweeping stone amphitheatre. This is Our Dynamic Earth, an interactive museum telling the story of our planet using special effects and interactive technology.

A visit to Our Dynamic Earth lasts around 90 minutes and first concentrates on the creation of life; a "time machine" takes you back to witness meteor showers, followed by the image of a barren, newly formed planet. Volcanoes erupt, the earth moves and shakes, sulphurous smells are all around and you can experience the cold of the

polar extremes. Other areas concentrate on the evolution of life and the oceans, and you can visit a tropical rainforest, where the air is damp and full of squawks and chatters of unseen animals and birds. Every 15 minutes the sky darkens, lightning flashes, thunder roars and sheets of torrential rain pour down. In the FutureDome you can take your crew seat as a time traveller and discover what the future holds for our planet.

Outside you can take in Earthscape Scotland, an external gallery where you can do some fossil rubbing. This is also a great place to have a picnic.

The many interactive computer programs and information boards are suitable for younger children. There are dinosaurs and dodos, a submarine "trip" to view ocean life, giant screens showing the glowing hues of the Northern Lights and much information on ecology. This is a great visit for all the family, with all information presented with the emphasis very much on learning through fun.

➕ 11D ✉ Holyrood Road, Holyrood ☎ 0131 550 7800
🕐 Daily 10:30–5. Closed 24, 25 Dec. Last entry 70 mins before closing 👖 Expensive 🍴 Cafe (£) 🚌 35, 36

7 Palace of Holyroodhouse

www.royalcollection.org.uk

The Queen's official Scottish residence, set against the background of Arthur's Seat, stands at the eastern end of the historic Royal Mile.

The Palace of Holyroodhouse is on the site of the original guest house for the medieval Holyrood Abbey, and is used today by Queen Elizabeth II as her home and office whenever she is in Edinburgh.

In 1501 James IV built a four-floor corner tower with gabled roof and balustrade, the existing northwest tower. Later additions were damaged and burned in 1544 and again in 1650. The palace attained its present form in 1671, when William Bruce designed an Italian-style courtyard quadrangle around which he built today's elegant structure. He fronted it by a tower matching the surviving medieval one, to which it is linked by an

entrance screen. The State Apartments, on the south side of the courtyard, include the Royal Dining Room, the Morning Drawing Room and the Throne Room. Across the court, the north range contains the Picture Gallery, decorated with portraits of 111 Scottish kings and queens from King Fergus in the 4th century to James VII, imaginatively created to order by Jacob de Wet.

Holyroodhouse has historical associations with many monarchs, among them James II, James IV and Charles II, while "Bonnie" Prince Charlie held

receptions here in the heady early days of the 1745 Jacobite Uprising. The memory of Mary, Queen of Scots is perhaps the most vivid; it was in her second-floor rooms that her secretary, David Rizzio, was stabbed to death in 1566 by her second husband, Lord Darnley, and his conspirators.

Be sure to visit the remains of Holyrood Abbey (➤ 103).

✚ 11C ✉ Canongate, Royal Mile ☎ 0131 556 5100
🕓 Apr–Oct daily 9:30–6; Nov–Mar 9:30–4:30. Last entry 45 mins before closing. Opening times may change at short notice – check online 🖐 Expensive 🚌 35, 36 ❓ Winter exhibitions from the Royal Collections, Nov–Mar

8 Royal Botanic Garden

www.rbge.org.uk

The Royal Botanic Garden's collections of trees, shrubs and flowers are an oasis of quiet, and draw plantsmen and garden lovers from many countries.

The garden started life in 1670 with the founding of a Physic Garden near the Palace of Holyroodhouse; three centuries later the garden is a thriving and internationally famous plant study base, and a haven of colour and scent throughout the year.

Moved to its present site in 1823, the garden covers 28ha (69 acres) of undulating ground lying between the city centre and the Firth of Forth. Winding paths link the different sections of the garden, much of which is grassed and dotted with the superb trees that comprise the Arboretum, a

ROYAL
BOTANIC
GARDEN
EDINBURGH

collection of more than 2,000 tree species, carpeted in spring with delicate spreads of bulbs. Spring flowers give way to rhododendrons and azaleas, their flaming reds and yellows offset by underplanting of lilies, primulas and *meconopsis*. The Rock Garden is at its best in late spring, its rocky slopes brilliant with Mediterranean and alpine plants, while the Heath Garden has year-round displays of Scottish and other heathers. High summer sees the 165m (180yd) herbaceous border, with its stately beech hedge at its best, and the rose collections fill the air with scent. Horticulturalists will be fascinated by the Chinese Hillside garden, where wild plants clothe the slopes of a watery ravine leading to a pond.

The Royal Botanic Garden is particularly famous for its glasshouses, a complex of ten contrasting structures where you'll find everything from Amazonian rainforest plants to cacti from deserts all over the world. Don't miss the Temperate Palm House, an elegant cast-iron structure built in 1858, and still the tallest in Britain.

✚ *Greater City 4c* ✉ 20A Inverleith Row
☎ 0131 552 7171 🕐 Apr–Sep daily 10–7; Mar, Oct 10–6; Nov–Feb 10–4 💷 Garden: free; glasshouses: moderate 🍽 Cafe and snack-bar (£–££)
🚌 8, 17, 23, 27

9 Royal Mile

Royal Mile runs downhill from Edinburgh Castle to Holyrood Palace and provides a focal point in the Old Town.

The vibrant, noisy streets of the Royal Mile are the tourist hub of Edinburgh. Thronged with people, lined with medieval tenements, packed with gift shops, and frequently echoing to the sounds of the bagpipes, this is the first port of call for every visitor. From the main thoroughfare, enticing closes (passageways) and wynds (narrow lanes) lead off between the buildings; discovering these is an essential part of exploring the Mile. Start at the top, where the solid bulk of the castle stands above the Esplanade with its splendid views, and work your way down to Holyrood, an area crammed with history, described by author Daniel Defoe as "the largest, longest and finest street…in the world".

Starting from the Esplanade look for Ramsay Gardens, an 18th-century baronial complex at the top of Castlehill. Past the Tolbooth St John's Kirk, now the Edinburgh Festival Hub (➤ 82–83), fine 16th- and 17th-century tenements line The Lawnmarket (➤ 85).

A nearby close was home to Deacon Brodie, this city worthy led a double life as a burglar and was hanged in 1788 outside St Giles' Cathedral (➤ 90–91), which stands at the top of the High Street. Opposite the cathedral, the City Chambers stand on the site of Mary King's Close, a medieval street which was blocked off during the Great Plague of 1645, its inhabitants left to die. Farther down, are more fine 16th-century buildings and a pub, the World's End, whose name commemorates the old city boundary. Below the High Street the Mile becomes Canongate, named after the Augustinian monks whose monastery once stood here. High points include Canongate Kirk dating from 1688. More attractive houses herald the approach to the Scottish Parliament building and the Palace of Holyroodhouse (➤ 48–49).

✚ 7E ✉ Royal Mile 🍴 Caffè Lucano (£–££; ➤ 65) or Deacon Brodie's Tavern (➤ 72) 🚌 23, 27, 35, 41, 42

DEACON BRODIES

10 Scott Monument

www.cac.org.uk

Fine views to the castle and Princes Street from one of the most grandiose memorials to a writer ever built, make the climb well worth while.

Worn out with excessive work in an attempt to pay off his creditors and those of his bankrupt publishers and printers, Sir Walter Scott died at his home, Abbotsford, in 1832. He was regarded by his contemporaries as one of Scotland's greatest writers, and no time was lost in erecting a fitting monument to his genius. The architect was George Meikle Kemp, a self-taught draughtsman, who won a competition for the memorial's design in 1838. The 200ft (61m) monument went up between 1840 and 1846, a riot of ornate Gothicism with a seated statue of Scott beneath the central vault. In contrast to the sandstone of the building, the statue is carved from white Carrara marble, the block from which it was sculpted happily having survived falling into Livorno harbour on its way from Italy to Leith. Scott is shown draped in plaid, with his favourite deerhound, Maida. The monument's 64 niches contain statues that represent many of the characters from Scott's works – fans of the Waverley novels can identify their favourites.

Climb right to the top of the Monument for sweeping views over the city; your ticket price includes a certificate to prove that you really did it. If the prospect of the 287 steps seems rather

daunting, you could go as far as the first level only.
Here you'll find a small room that displays
information about Scott's life and work, and there
are also headphones which you can use to listen to
readings and musical settings of his novels.

✚ 6D ✉ East Princes Street Gardens ☎ 0131 529 4068
🕐 Apr–Sep Mon–Sat 9–6; Oct–Mar daily 10–4
✋ Moderate 🍴 Refreshment kiosk in East Princes
Gardens (£) 🚌 23, 27, 41 and others to Princes Street

Best things to do

Great places to have lunch

Cramond Inn (£–££)

A British-style pub in the heart of old Cramond. Hearty lunches; family friendly.

 Cramond Glebe Road ☎ 0131 336 2035

Daniel's Bistro (££)

This French-style bistro with strong Scottish overtones serves good food in a pretty conservatory setting.

✉ 88 Commercial Street, Leith ☎ 0131 553 5933

Filmhouse Café (£)

This art-house cinema cafe provides an ideal place to have a quick hot or cold snack, either before a movie or not.

✉ 88 Lothian Road ☎ 0131 229 5932

Henderson's at St John's (£)

A great spot for a vegetarian lunch. Right at the heart of the city in a dramatic setting.

✉ St John's Church, Lothian Road/Princes Street
☎ 0131 229 0212

Kay's Bar (£)

A cosy New Town pub serving straightforward, good-value pub food.

✉ 39 Jamaica Street West ☎ 0131 225 1858

Mussel and Steak Bar (£)

Enjoy a plate of plump Shetland mussels before indulging in some perfectly cooked Scottish beef.

✉ 110 West Bow,
The Grassmarket
☎ 0131 225 5028

The Rutland (££)
A chic hotel/restaurant at
the west end of Princes
Street with some views
of the castle and outside
tables in summer.
✉ 1–3 Rutland Street
☎ 0131 229 3402

The Shore Bar and Restaurant (££)
Dine on excellent
seafood overlooking the
Water of Leith.
✉ 3 Shore, Leith
☎ 0131 553 5000

Valvona and Crolla (££)
Enjoy pizzas, pasta and
authentic dishes in a truly
Italian deli atmosphere.
✉ 19 Elm Row
☎ 0131 556 6066

Wee Windaes (££)
Perfectly placed on the
Royal Mile for a traditional
Scottish lunch.
✉ 144 High Street
☎ 0131 225 5144

Best buys

Bagpipes: you may not be able to afford the full-size real thing, but there are plenty of small versions to buy.

Books, prints and maps: a wide choice at city bookshops and antiquarian specialists.

Cashmere and wool: top prices for the softest and silkiest items of cashmere plus more humble pure wool options.

Celtic jewellery: lovely items in silver can be found in the traditional jewellery shops in town.

Edinburgh shortbread: track down Scotland's national sweet treat from one of the specialist producers.

Edinburgh Rock: this super-sweet, multi-hued rock differs from others in its variety of flavours and its soft consistency. It comes in sticks and bite-size chunks.

Edinburgh crystal: ranges from delicate drinking ware to dazzling paperweights, ships' decanters and elegant bowls and vases.

Kilts and tartans: there are plenty to choose from on the Royal Mile, made-to-measure, off-the-peg or just a tartan gift to take home.

Whisky: where else to buy the national drink and nectar to the Scots?

Places to take the children

Brass Rubbing Centre
Children of all ages can try their hand at rubbing brasses from the centre's large collection of replica brasses.
✉ Trinity Apse, Chalmers Close, off Royal Mile ☎ 0131 556 4364; www.edinburgh.co.uk ⏱ Apr–Oct Mon–Sat 10–5 🚌 3, 7, 14, 33, 35

Butterfly and Insect World
Colourful and spectacular butterflies together with fascinating insects, all in a rainforest habitat. Regular mini-beast handlings.
✉ Dobbies Garden World, Lasswade ☎ 0131 663 4932; www.edinburgh-butterfly-world.co.uk ⏱ Apr–Oct daily 9:30–5:30; Nov–Mar 10–5 🚌 3, 29

Dalkeith Country Park
Parklands with waymarked walks, livestock and exciting Woodland Adventure area to explore.
✉ Dalkeith ☎ 0131 654 1666; www.dalkeithcountryestate.com
⏱ Apr–Sep daily 10–5:30 🚌 3, 3A, 49

Edinburgh Dungeon
Lurking in the depths of historic Edinburgh you will find ghosts, vampires, body-snatchers and more. Not for the faint hearted or young.
✉ 32 Market Street ☎ 0131 240 1000; www.the-dungeons.co.uk ⏱ 1 Jan–20 Mar Mon–Fri 11–4, Sat–Sun 10:30–4:30; 21 Mar–25 Jun daily 10–5; 26 Jun–30 Aug daily 10–7; 31 Aug–1 Nov daily 10–5; 31 Oct 10–8; 2 Nov–31 Dec Mon–Fri 11–4, Sat–Sun 11–5 🚌 36 and all to Waverley station 💷 Expensive

Edinburgh Zoo
See page 146.

Hard Rock Café
This original themed restaurant may be brash and noisy, but the burgers are good and the fries popular with young ones.
✉ 20 George Street ☎ 0131 260 3000; www.hardrock.com ⏱ Daily food 12–11; bar closes at 1am 🚌 19, 23, 41

Laser Quest
Arcade and computer games systems, plus the ultimate laser game, stalking an opponent through a smoke-filled battle zone.
✉ 56B Dalry Road ☎ 0131 346 1919; www.laserquest-edinburgh.co.uk ⏱ Mon–Sat 11–11; Sun 11–8 🚌 2, 3, 4, 25, 33

Leith Waterworld
A state-of-the-art leisure pool at the foot of Easter Road with a wide range of facilities, wave machine and water flume.
✉ 377 Easter Road ☎ 0131 555 6000; www.edinburghleisure.co.uk ⏱ Edinburgh school hols Fri 10:30–4:45, Sat–Thu 10–4:45; term time Fri 10:30–4:45, Sat–Sun 10–4:45 🚌 1, 13, 35

Maid of the Forth
Enjoy a spectacular cruise from beneath the historic Forth Rail Bridge, with visits to the abbey on Inchcolm Island and close encounters with seals and dolphins (► 28, 181).
✉ Hawes Pier, South Queensferry ☎ 0131 331 5000 (for sailing times); www.maidoftheforth.co.uk ⏱ Easter–Oct 🚌 First Bus 43

Witchery Tour
Older children will be enthralled by the Ghost and Gore, or Murder and Mystery tours through the darker parts of Old Edinburgh.
✉ 84 West Bow ☎ 0131 225 6745; www.witcherytours.com 🚌 23, 27, 35, 41, 42

a walk along the Royal Mile

Start at the Castle Esplanade and head down Castlehill passing the Scotch Whisky Heritage Centre (➤ 91) on your right and the Camera Obscura and World of Illusions (➤ 79) on your left. Continue to the Tolbooth Church, now the Edinburgh Festival Hub (➤ 82–83), and cross the road into The Lawnmarket (➤ 85).

Wander through some of the quiet closes leading off The Lawnmarket to escape the crowds and soak up the 200-year-old atmosphere.

Cross the street at the junction where The Lawnmarket becomes the High Street and is bisected by North Bank Street and George IV Bridge.

The ornate domed building at the bottom of the slope to your left is the headquarters of the Bank of Scotland, first built in 1802 and redesigned by David Bryce in 1864.

Continue downhill, passing Parliament Square (➤ 89) and St Giles' Cathedral (➤ 90–91) on your right.

Opposite the cathedral, an impressive

Edwardian baroque complex houses the City Chambers, (1898–1904).

Continue to the Tron Kirk (▶ 109) on the corner of the Bridges. Cross the road and walk to the bottom of the High Street and cross St Mary's Street into the Canongate stretch.

You'll find the Museum of Childhood (▶ 104–105) and John Knox House (▶ 104) as you approach the end of the High Street.

Walk down the Canongate.

This stretch has the Museum of Edinburgh and People's Story museum (▶ 106–107). At the bottom you'll see the Canongate facade of the Scottish Parliament.

Cross Abbey Strand to reach the gates of the Palace of Holyroodhouse (▶ 48–49).

Distance 1.8km (1.1 miles)
Time 30 minutes without stops, 3–6 hours with museum visits
Start Point Castle Esplanade ✚ 14H 🚌 23, 27, 41, 42
End Point Palace of Holyroodhouse ✚ 11C 🚌 35
Lunch Caffè Lucano (£–££) ✉ 37–39 St George IV Bridge
☎ 0131 225 6690

Top activities

Walking: join one of the themed guided walks through Edinburgh's historic Old Town (➤ 100) or take a hike up Arthur's Seat (➤ 36–37).

Cycling: city cycle lanes or miles of off-road cycle paths; just remember it's a hilly city.
✉ 276 Leith Walk ☎ 0131 467 7775; www.leithcycleco.com

Swimming: pools range from state-of-the-art water complexes to splendid Victorian baths. Edinburgh Leisure runs a variety of swimming pools around the city.
☎ 0131 458 2100; www.edinburghleisure.co.uk

Golf: a good range of courses at different prices. Edinburgh Leisure has six public courses – at Braid Hills (➤ 161), Carrick Knowe, Craigentinny, Portobello, Princes and Silverknowes.
☎ 0131 458 2100; www.edinburghleisure.co.uk

Rugby Union: impressive Murrayfield Stadium (➤ 148) to the west of the city centre is home to the Scottish national team, and venue for most international matches. Tours of the stadium are available.
✉ Corstorphine Road ☎ 0131 346 5000; www.murrayfieldexperience.com
🚌 12, 22, 26, 31

Ice skating: the rink next to the rugby stadium offers sessions for beginners and more accomplished skaters alike. The rink is also home to Edinbugh's ice hockey team, the Edinburgh Capitals.
☎ 0131 337 6933; www.murrayfieldicerinkltd.co.uk

Skiing: Europe's longest artificial ski slope is just south of the city, with chairlift facilities for skiers, snowboarders and sightseers.
✉ Biggar Road, Hillend ☎ 0131 445 4433; www.midlothian.gov.uk
🚌 4, 15, 15A

Tennis: you'll find courts at parks and private clubs across the city and surrounding area. Alternatively Edinburgh Leisure operates several courts and offers coaching courses for all abilities.
☎ 0131 458 2100; www.edinburghleisure.co.uk

Watersports: head for South Queensferry to try dinghy sailing or canoeing (➤ 181) or take a boat trip; the *Forth Belle* offers cruises throughout the year (➤ 28).
☎ 087 0118 1866; www.forthboattours.com

Helicopter flights: get a bird's-eye view of Edinburgh on a guided tour. Lothian Helicopter offers a selection of flights over the city and surrounding area.
☎ 0131 228 9999; www.lothianhelicopters.co.uk

Stunning views

From the top of Arthur's Seat (▶ 36–37) well worth the climb.

Spend time on the ramparts of Edinburgh Castle (▶ 38–39) looking at Princes Street and the New Town to the north.

From Calton Hill (▶ 114) a sweeping vista towards Princes Street and the castle.

Stand in the New Town (▶ 44–45) and experience the grandeur of Georgian town planning.

Drive out to South Queensferry to view the splendour of the two Forth bridges from below and the wide Firth of Forth.

Climb the Scott Monument (▶ 54–55) for superb views along Princes Street, up the Mound and over towards the castle.

Stand in Melville Street and admire its spacious elegance dominated by the spires of St Mary's.

Don't miss the roof-terrace view at the National Museum of Scotland (➤ 40–41).

Blackford Hill (➤ 140) gives wide views back towards the heart of the city and the Firth of Forth and Fife hills.

Stand at the corner of The Lawnmarket (➤ 85) and the High Street for the best view of the Royal Mile.

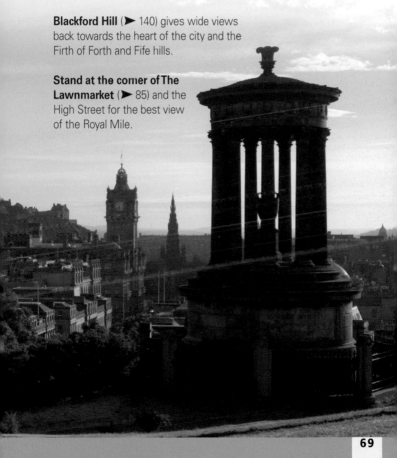

Splendid statues

Allan Ramsay in West Princes Street Gardens: the 18th-century poet carved from an 18-ton block of marble by Sir John Steel in 1865.
✚ D5

David Livingstone in East Princes Street Gardens: the 19th-century missionary and explorer sculpted in bronze by Amelia Robertson Hill in 1876.
✚ D5

John Knox in Parliament Square: commemorated by a bronze statue against the wall of St Giles, designed by Pittendrigh MacGillivray in 1906.
✚ E6

The Duke of Wellington in Princes Street: 12-ton bronze equestrian statue outside Register House; designed by Sir John Steele in 1832.
✚ C7

Charles II in Parliament Square: the city's oldest statue and Britain's oldest equestrian statue by an unknown sculptor, dated 1685.
✚ E6

Henry Dundas 1st Viscount Melville in St Andrew Square: this influential politician presides 41m (134ft) high on a column designed by William Burn in 1820.
✚ C6

Sherlock Holmes in Picardy Place (left): Britain's only statue of the fictional detective by John Doubleday, close to where his creator Sir Arthur Conan-Doyle lived.
✚ B8

Field Marshal Earl Haig at the bottom of Castlehill: the eminent World War I soldier sits astride his horse, a monument to the field marshal by George Wade.
✚ E5

Robert the Bruce and William Wallace guard the entrance to the castle: the two Scottish icons represented in stone in castle wall niches created by T J Clapperton and William Carrick respectively in 1929.
✚ E5

Robert Burns in Bernard Street, Leith: the renowned poet sculpted in bronze by D W Stevenson and erected in 1898.
✚ (off map)

Best pubs

Baillie Bar
A traditional basement pub in Stockbridge serving good real ales. Interesting triangular-shaped bar, low ceilings and dark-red walls.
✉ 2–4 St Stephen Street ☎ 0131 225 4673

The Bow Bar
In the historic Old Town, this classic one-roomed pub serves eight cask ales and 150 malt whiskies dispensed from antique equipment. Bar snacks only.
✉ 80 The West Bow
☎ 0131 226 7667

Deacon Brodie's Tavern
Find out more about the infamous Brodie while you sup your pint. A traditional pub, with bar snacks downstairs, restaurant upstairs. A perfect refuelling stop on the Royal Mile.
✉ 35 Lawnmarket ☎ 0131 225 6531

The Ferry Tap
A characterful old local haunt on the pretty cobbled High Street in the relaxed waterfront suburb of South Queensferry. Fine ales, excellent whiskies and solid bar meals.
✉ 36 High Street, South Queensferry ☎ 0131 331 2000

Greyfriars Bobby
In front of Greyfriars Kirk and named after the famous loyal dog, this wooden-fronted building houses a traditional friendly pub that is very popular with students from the nearby university.
✉ 34 Candlemaker Row ☎ 0131 225 8328

Jolly Judge

You have to search to find the alley where this fine old pub is located. It's about as traditional as you can get with low ceilings, beams and a relaxed atmosphere. There's a fine range of ales and wide choice of whiskies.

✉ 7 James Court, off Lawnmarket ☎ 0131 225 2669

The Last Drop

An historic pub by the city's old gallows, with a lively mix of locals, tourists and students. It serves a good pint of heavy ale.

✉ 74–78 Grassmarket ☎ 0131 225 4851

Sheep's Heid Inn

You'll get a friendly welcome at the oldest pub in Edinburgh, located in Duddingston, on the edge of Holyrood Park. Good beer, tasty food and even a traditional skittle alley.

✉ 43–45 The Causeway, Duddingston ☎ 0131 656 6952

Starbank Inn

With great views over the River Forth, the pub offers four traditional cask-conditioned ales, four guest ales and a good selection of single malt whiskies. Dine on traditional home-cooked food in the conservatory. It's away from tourist Edinburgh, and feels it.

✉ 4 Laverockbank Road, Trinity ☎ 0131 552 4141

The Tass

A genuine traditional Scottish pub named after one of Rabbie Burns' songs, *The Silver Tassle*. Good range of beers, wines and whiskies, plus tasty home-cooked food. This is the place to come for traditional folk music sessions. A real oasis on the Royal Mile.

✉ Corner of High Street and St Mary's Street ☎ 0131 556 6338

Exploring

For many Scots, the Edinburgh of today seems more like a true capital city than it has for almost 300 years, since it is now the place where the Scottish Parliament sits to determine many of the issues affecting the country's people.

The city has enjoyed wonderful architecture and fine museums for many years; in this, the third millennium, it does so with a sound economy, growing prosperity and a clutch of new buildings and enterprises. It offers excellent exhibition and conference facilities, its financial institutions are of international importance and the research carried out in its universities is renowned worldwide. Increasingly a truly cosmopolitan city, with a cultural life whose dynamism is no longer confined to August and the Festival, Edinburgh rates highly for the quality of life enjoyed by its citizens and those who come to visit.

Old Town

This district epitomizes "auld" Edinburgh, steeped in history and dominated by the formidable fortification, Edinburgh Castle.

Visit the castle to learn more of the history of the city and be sure not to miss it lit up at night. In the Old Town you can explore the tiny alleys known as wynds that branch out from the main thoroughfare, the Royal Mile, which stretches down to the Palace of Holyroodhouse. At the Old Town end this road is made up of Castlehill, Lawnmarket and the High Street with specialist shops, traditional pubs and a mix of cosmopolitan restaurants. This was the area where, until the building of the New Town in the 18th century, all classes of society lived cheek by jowl. After the new building the working classes were left to inhabit the tenement buildings and the narrow alleys, now seen as a historic visitor attraction.

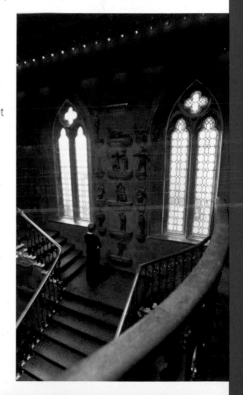

CAMERA OBSCURA AND WORLD OF ILLUSIONS

The camera obscura, invented in the 19th century, uses mirrors to project images of the outside world on to lenses and thus to a white disk. The lenses rotate 360 degrees, giving a bird's-eye view. It's a fair climb up to Edinburgh's Camera Obscura, but you can pause at the hologram exhibition to get your breath. Go on a clear day as the camera depends on natural light and you won't see so much if it's gloomy.

www.camera-obscura.co.uk

➕ 15H ✉ Castlehill, Royal Mile ☎ 0131 226 3709 🕐 Apr–Jun daily 9:30–7; Jul–Aug 9:30–7:30; Sep–Oct 9:30–6; Nov–Mar 10–5 💷 Expensive
🚌 23, 27, 35, 41, 42

COWGATE

The long street called the Cowgate, now an upmarket part of the Old Town, runs canyon-like beneath the South and George IV bridges, and connects The Grassmarket (➤ 84) with the Canongate area of the Old Town. Through here, in medieval times, cattle were driven from the plots behind the High Street houses to pasture outside the walls, hence the name. By 1500 the Cowgate had become Edinburgh's first fashionable suburb, lined with the houses of rich merchants and the aristocracy. Centuries later, it housed Edinburgh's large Irish community and the city's breweries. Look for **St Cecilia's Hall;** built in 1763, this was the city's first concert venue. The building of the new Scottish Parliament, and the opening of new bars and clubs has revitalized the area.

➕ 16–18H ✉ Cowgate 🚌 8, 35, 41, 42

St Cecilia's Hall

✉ Cowgate ☎ 0131 650 2805 ❓ Concert venue for University of Edinburgh

EDINBURGH CASTLE

Best places to see, ➤ 38–39.

EDINBURGH CASTLE MUSEUMS

Besides its ramparts, batteries, courtyards and fine buildings, **Edinburgh Castle** (➤ 38–39) also houses an interesting museum, mainly connected with Scotland's military past. Though not strictly a museum, the Scottish National War Memorial draws thousands of visitors to admire its austere splendours. Designed by Robert Lorimer in 1924, it first commemorated the more than 100,000 Scots who died in World War I. Nearby is the **National War Museum of Scotland,** a military museum devoted to the uniforms and equipment of the armed forces in the country. Sections are devoted to the Royal Navy and the Royal Air Force. There are no less than nine Victoria Crosses on display, together with a mass of paintings, photos and general military ephemera as well as personal items and weapons. On the castle rampart is Mons Meg, a huge cannon built in Belgium and presented in the 15th century to James II as one of a pair.

Edinburgh Castle

✚ 13H ✉ Edinburgh Castle, Castle Hill ☎ 0131 225 9846
⊕ ➤ 38–39 💷 Expensive 🍴 Restaurant and cafe (£–££)
🚌 23, 27, 35, 41, 42

National War Museum of Scotland

☎ 0131 247 4413; www.nms.ac.uk ⊕ Apr–Sep daily 9:45–5:45; Oct–Mar 9:45–4:45 💷 Included in castle entry

EDINBURGH EXCHANGE

It's well worth walking up the Lothian Road and along the West Approach Road to take a look at the £350-million-plus development known as the Edinburgh Exchange, the new financial district. The development plan was launched in 1988, after the construction of the palatial Sheraton Grand on what was then the rather run-down lower reaches of Lothian Road. Impressive buildings have gone up, grouped around the Edinburgh International Conference Centre, opened in 1995 and designed by Terry Farrell. Building continues but the existing monuments to late 20th-century commerce, all soaring brick, stone and glass, are impressive enough. Worth noticing are the Standard Life building on Lothian Road, with its fine gates and railings, and the impressive Scottish Widows building on Morrison Street.

✚ 2⊦ ✉ Lothian Road and West Approach Road 🚌 1, 10, 11, 22

EDINBURGH'S FESTIVAL CENTRE – THE HUB

More than 50 years after the first Edinburgh Festival, and nearly 33 after moving into "temporary" headquarters, in 1999 the Festival offices finally moved into a purpose-designed suite in the magnificently converted Tolbooth at the top of the Royal Mile. The exterior, designed by Augustus Pugin for the Church of Scotland in the 1840s, remains unchanged, while inside you'll find some of Scotland's most exciting and innovative contemporary design. Sculptures, lighting, textiles and tiling make the mundane act of

buying a ticket part of the Festival experience. The Hub is open year-round and provides a "taste of the Festival" no matter when you come, with information and tickets on all the city's festivals throughout the year (▶ 24–25), a hall and library, restaurant, shop and other facilities.

www.thehub-edinburgh.com

✚ 15H ✉ Castle Hill, Royal Mile ☎ 0131 473 2015; Café Hub 0131 473 2067 🕓 8am–11pm 👍 Free 🍴 Café Hub (£–££) 🚍 23, 27, 35, 41, 42

GLADSTONE'S LAND

Gladstone's Land, a narrow, six-floor arcaded building and Edinburgh's finest surviving high-level tenement, was purchased in 1617 by Thomas Gledstanes, a merchant and burgess. The prosperous Gledstanes family remodelled the prestigiously placed house, using the arcaded ground floor as a shop, and letting all but one of the other floors, which Thomas retained for his own use. Today, the ground-floor booths display 17th-century wares, while the rooms on the first floor are furnished as the typical home of a wealthy citizen of that time. The main bedroom has a beautiful painted ceiling, decorated with fruit and flowers, and traces of the original frescoes on the walls. The Gladstone Gallery has changing exhibitions of contemporary local artists.

www.nts.org.uk

✚ 6E ✉ 477B Lawnmarket, Royal Mile ☎ 0131 226 5856 🕓 Apr–Jun, Sep, Oct daily 10–5; Jul, Aug 10–7 👍 Moderate, but free to National Trust and National Trust for Scotland members 🚍 23, 27, 35, 41, 42

THE GRASSMARKET

Crouched below the Castle Rock, the long open space known as The Grassmarket is one of old Edinburgh's most attractive squares. With its cobbled pathways and groups of trees it has a French atmosphere and makes a pleasant place to pause for a little window shopping and a drink at one of its bars or pubs. Over the years it has been used for various activities. It was first chartered as a market in 1477 and served for more than 300 years as the city's main corn and livestock market, besides being the site of the local gallows. The Covenanters' Memorial commemorates the many citizens who were hanged here during the religious upheavals of the 17th century. The Grassmarket has been considerably smartened up in recent years, but manages to retain something of the atmosphere Robert Burns must have felt when he wrote *Ae Fond Kiss* in the White Hart Inn.

➕ 15J ✉ The Grassmarket 🚌 2, 35, 41, 42

GREYFRIARS KIRK

Historic Greyfriars Kirk, standing on the site of a Franciscan friary, was built in 1620, a simple and peaceful church surrounded by a green kirkyard, the site of the signing of the National Covenant in 1638 (➤ 91). Most visitors come here to see the statue of a small Skye terrier on a fountain opposite the churchyard gate. The statue commemorates Greyfriars Bobby, a loyal dog who kept watch here at his master's grave for 14 years until his own death in 1872.

➕ 16J ✉ 2 Greyfriars Place, Candlemaker Row ☎ 0131 226 5429
🕐 Easter–Oct Mon–Fri 10:30–4:30, Sat 10:30–2:30 ✋ Free 🚌 2, 23, 27, 35, 41, 42

THE HEART OF MIDLOTHIAN

Stand with your back to the entrance to St Giles' Cathedral and move about 20 paces forward and slightly to your right. At your feet you'll see the outline of a heart laid out in cobblestones.

This is the Heart of Midlothian, which marks the place of the 15th-century Tolbooth prison, where executions took place. In the past, locals would spit on the spot, and some still do.

✚ 6E ✉ High Street 🍴 Jackson's (ff–fff; ➤ 96) 🚌 23, 27, 35, 41, 42

THE LAWNMARKET

The Lawnmarket is the name given to the section of the Royal Mile below Castlehill and above the High Street. It is one of the oldest streets in Edinburgh, and originally formed the 12th-century nucleus of David I's burgh. Its name comes from the "lawn" or cloth once sold here and by the late 17th century it was the smartest place to live. Running off The Lawnmarket are some of the Old Town's best examples of closes and vennels. There are three entrances to James's Court, an 18th-century close, once the home of David Hume, the philosopher, and James Boswell, Dr Johnson's biographer. Milne's Court, to the west, went up in 1690, a planned development to try to ease the congestion in the Old Town. Look out, too, for Brodie's Close, home to the notorious Deacon Brodie.

✚ 15–16H ✉ The Lawnmarket 🚌 23, 27, 28, 35, 41, 42

THE MEADOWS

The open grassy space of Meadow Park is known as The Meadows. Criss-crossed with paths and studded with trees, it is popular with students from the university, doctors and nurses from the nearby Royal Infirmary and families from the surrounding residential streets. It's a good place to relax or let children run about, and there's a playground with slides and swings. The whole area was once covered by the Burgh Loch, which supplied Edinburgh's water. Piped water arrived in 1676, the loch was drained in the 18th century and The Meadows became a public park in 1860. Twenty-six years later the grand International Exhibition of Industry was held here; the Whalebone Arch is a relic of this. Enjoy The Meadows by day, but its unlit paths are better avoided at night.

✚ 15M ✉ The Meadows 🚍 3, 3A, 5, 7, 31

MERCAT CROSS

Spare a few moments as you walk down Royal Mile to admire the Mercat Cross outside St Giles. It is one of the most evocative symbols of Edinburgh. Today's version dates from the 1880s and is modelled on the 17th-century cross; it was restored in 1970 and again in 1990, when the eight medallions showing the arms of Britain, Scotland, England and Ireland and another four connected with Edinburgh were gilded. In medieval times the Mercat Cross was the focus for trade, and there's probably been a cross on this site since the 12th century. Public festivities took place here, royal proclamations were read, and executions performed. In 1513 the troops set out from here on the fateful march to defeat at the Battle of Flodden.

✚ 7E ✉ High Street 🚌 23, 27, 35, 41, 42

NATIONAL MUSEUM OF SCOTLAND

Best places to see, ➤ 40–41.

PARLIAMENT HOUSE

From 1639 until the Treaty of Union in 1707 the Scots Parliament met in Parliament House, a superb 17th-century Scottish Renaissance building just behind St Giles' Cathedral. The long and lofty main chamber, Parliament Hall, was home to the "Three Estates" – no distinction was made in Scotland between clergy, nobility and burgesses. Scottish MPs processed from here in July 1999 before the opening of the new Scottish Parliament Building (➤ 108). The hall has a magnificent hammerbeam roof and a fine 19th-century stained-glass window. The building is now occupied by law courts and advocates' chambers, and there's an interesting display on its history and present use.

✚ 16H ✉ Parliament Square ☎ 0131 225 2595 ❸ Mon–Fri 9–4:30
✋ Free 🚌 23, 27, 35, 41, 42

PARLIAMENT SQUARE

Parliament Square, lying behind St Giles' Cathedral, is an open space surrounded by the 19th-century colonnades masking Parliament House; they were designed by Robert Reid and built between 1803 and 1830. The equestrian statue of Charles II excited much comment when it went up in 1685, Roman triumphal dress being less than familiar to the locals. You'll see lawyers hurrying through the square on their way to the Court of Session and the High Court of Justice.

✚ 16H ✉ Parliament Square 🚌 23, 27, 35, 41, 42

THE REAL MARY KING'S CLOSE

Beneath Royal Mile lies a warren of narrow medieval streets, covered when the City Chambers were constructed during the 1750s. The houses along here had been tall tenements; some were knocked down to create space, others incorporated into the foundations of the City Chambers, the rest bricked up and forgotten. You can now explore this hidden world, guided by characters based on the people who lived there. The tour takes in some fine 17th-century houses, a sawmaker's shop and the home of a gravedigger where you find out about the 1644 plague.

www.realmarykingsclose.co.uk

✚ 6E ✉ 2 Warriston's Close, High Street ☎ 08702 430160 🕐 Apr–Oct daily 10–9 (Aug 9–9); Nov–Mar Sun–Fri 10–5, Sat 10–9 💷 Expensive 🚌 23, 28, 35, 41, 42

ROYAL MILE

Best places to see, ➤ 52–53.

ST GILES' CATHEDRAL

St Giles' Cathedral, the High Kirk of Edinburgh, dates mainly from
the 14th and 15th centuries. The oldest parts of the church are the
four massive columns surrounding the Holy Table in the crossing;
these support the central lantern, with its flying buttresses and
spire, raised in 1500. The original cruciform church was widened by
the construction of extra chapels; the choir, which dates to 1419, is
among the finest pieces of medieval architecture in Scotland.
Another highlight is the Thistle Chapel, an exquisite Gothic Revival
masterpiece designed by Robert Lorimer in 1909 for the Knights of
the chivalric Order of the Thistle. St Giles was John Knox's church;
here he preached until his death in 1572, struggling to establish
Presbyterianism as Scotland's faith during the reign of Mary, Queen
of Scots. Here, too, the religious disturbances of 1637 began when

the new Prayer Book, similar to the English Prayer Book, was introduced; this led to the signing of the National Covenant abolishing Episcopacy.
www.stgilescathedral.org.uk
✚ 6E ✉ Parliament Square, High Street
☎ 0131 225 9442 🕐 May–Sep Mon–Fri 9–7, Sat 9–5, Sun 1–6; Oct–Apr Mon–Sat 9–5, Sun 1–5 ✋ Free, donation for entrance to Thistle Chapel 🚌 23, 27, 28, 35, 41, 42

SCOTCH WHISKY HERITAGE CENTRE

Scotland's national drink is the theme of this entertaining and informative visitor centre, which attracts people from all over the world. If you want to learn about the history, manufacture and blending of whisky, head here. The introduction to the tour takes you through the different processes in the production of Scotch whisky. You'll learn about the different whisky regions and the effect of local conditions on the taste and "nose" of the spirit, with a chance to have a sniff yourself. You'll meet the resident ghost, the Master Blender, then take a ride in a barrel-car through 300 years of whisky history, complete with scents and sounds. The on-site restaurant is excellent.

www.whisky-heritage.co.uk
✚ 15H ✉ 354 Castlehill, Royal Mile ☎ 0131 220 0441 🕐 Jun–Aug daily 9:30–6:30; Sep–May 10–6 (last tour 1 hour before closing) ✋ Expensive
🍴 Restaurant and bar (££)
🚌 23, 27, 35, 41, 42
❓ Tour includes free dram of whisky; around 270 varieties for sale in shop

TALBOT RICE GALLERY

The Talbot Rice Gallery, a huge and airy balconied building that opened in 1975, lies just off the Old Quad of the University of Edinburgh. It houses the Torrie Collection, a pleasing small collection of Dutch and Italian Old Masters. The gallery is probably better known for its changing exhibitions, which run all year round, with shows by established Scottish and other artists.

www.trg.ed.ac.uk

✛ 17J ✉ Old College, South Bridge ☎ 0131 650 2210; 🕓 Tue–Sat 10–5; daily during Festival ✋ Free, but charges for some exhibitions 🚌 3, 7, 14, 33

UNIVERSITY OF EDINBURGH

The University of Edinburgh was founded in 1582. Its buildings are grouped around Old College, designed by Robert Adam in 1789. Nearby lies George Square, home to the arts and science departments, with a few fine Georgian houses still huddled beneath the monstrous 1960s campus building. The McEwan Hall is used for ceremonial occasions, while the Classical Reid Concert Hall also houses the Historic Instrument Collection. You can visit several of the university's buildings: The Playfair Library, one of Edinburgh's finest Classical interiors, is the pick of the bunch.

www.ed.ac.uk

✛ 16J and 17K ✉ University of Edinburgh Centre, 7–11 Nicolson Street ☎ 0131 650 2252 🕓 Mon–Fri 9:30–4:30. Closed Wed 12:30–1:30 ✋ Free 🚌 7, 8, 14, 33

VICTORIA STREET

The steep curve of Victoria Street links The Grassmarket with George IV Bridge and the Royal Mile. It's a cobbled street lined with some of Edinburgh's most individual stores. As you walk down, look up to your right at the old tenements clinging to the slopes beneath Royal Mile. This area is the West Bow, once

the processional way into the Old Town, and the former route from Castlehill to The Grassmarket. Walk along Victoria Terrace to experience the atmosphere of this part of town.

✚ 15–16H ✉ Victoria Street 🚌 23, 27, 35, 41, 42

THE WRITERS' MUSEUM

The Writers' Museum occupies a three-floor house on Lady Stair's Close, which was built in 1622 by a merchant whose daughter made it over to Lady Stair in 1719. (Lady Stair was the widow of the judge and Secretary of State John Dalrymple, 1st Earl of Stair, who was held largely responsible for the massacre of Glencoe.) The museum is devoted to Scotland's great trio – Robert Burns, Sir Walter Scott and Robert Louis Stevenson. There's much well-presented information on the lives and works of these writers in the form of memorabilia, documents and pictures, with sound guides to help you make the most of your visit. The museum also stages temporary exhibitions on aspects of the writers' lives.

www.cac.org.uk

✚ 6E ✉ Lady Stair's Close, The Lawnmarket, Royal Mile ☎ 0131 529 4901 🕐 Mon–Sat 10–5; also Sun 12–5 during Edinburgh Festival ✋ Free 🚌 23, 27, 35, 41 ❓ Changing temporary exhibitions on literary themes

HOTELS

Apex International (££)

This excellent-value city-centre hotel offers good, international-standard accommodation in family-size en-suite rooms, with the bonus of a rooftop restaurant.

✉ 31–35 Grassmarket ☎ 0131 300 3456; www.apexhotels.co.uk
🚌 2, 35

Edinburgh Central Premier Travel Inn (£)

The city's newest Premier Travel Inn provides basic but perfectly comfortable accommodation just a short stroll from the Grassmarket and the rest of Old Town's attractions.

✉ 82 Lauriston Place ☎ 0870 990 6610 🚌 2, 35

Missoni (£££)

Opened in 2009, this seriously chic luxury design hotel is already a favourite with visiting celebrity A-listers and those looking to see and be seen. It has already staked a claim to be the most stylish hotel in the capital.

✉ 1 George IV Bridge ☎ 0131 220 6666; www.hotelmissoni.com
🚌 23, 27, 45

Radisson SAS (£££)

Located close to Holyrood Park, this big, stylish hotel offers a full range of international-class facilities, including a health club, swimming pool and sauna and is housed in a mock-medieval turreted building.

✉ 80 High Street, Royal Mile ☎ 0131 557 9797;
www.edinburgh.radissonsas.com 🚌 23, 27, 35, 41, 42

Town House (£–££)

Small, friendly Victorian hotel built in 1876, 15 minutes' walk from Princes Street. The five rooms are comfortable and retain period features, but they also offer WiFi. Try the authentic Scottish breakfast of porridge and local kippers.

✉ 65 Gilmore Place ☎ 0131 229 1985; www.thetownhouse.com
🚌 10, 27

RESTAURANTS

Atrium (£££)

A sophisticated, minimalist restaurant housed in the foyer of the Traverse Theatre (➤ 99).It has a high reputation with a distinctive range of imaginative Scottish and international dishes.

✉ 10 Cambridge Street ☎ 0131 228 8882; www.atriumrestaurant.co.uk

🕙 Mon–Fri 12–2, 6:30–10, Sat 6:30–10. Closed Sun 🚌 10, 11, 16, 22

Blue Bar Café (££)

This modern brasserie serves excellent food drawing on many influences from around the world. Light dishes and main meals made with the freshest of local produce.

✉ 10 Cambridge Street ☎ 0131 221 1222; www.bluescotland.co.uk

🕙 Mon–Thu 12–2:30, 5:30–10:30, Fri–Sat 12–2:30, 5:30–11

🚌 10, 11, 16, 22

Creelers (££–£££)

A long-established favourite, Creelers has two dining rooms, each attractively decked out, the back one for more intimate dining. You can almost taste the sea with the fine-quality fresh fish and seafood coming direct from the family-owned Arran Smokehouse.

✉ 3 Hunter Square ☎ 0131 220 4447; www.creelers.co.uk 🕙 Mon–Thu 12–2:30, 5:30–10:30, Fri 12–2:30, 5:30–11, Sat 12–3, 5:30–11, Sun 1–3, 6–10.30 🚌 23, 35, 41

Elephant House (£)

This popular, friendly cafe offers a wide range of light meals and snacks throughout the day, with a tempting array of cakes to complement the speciality coffees.

✉ 21 George IV Bridge ☎ 0131 220 5355; www.elephanthouse.biz

🕙 Mon–Fri 8am–11pm, Sat 10–11, Sun 10–10 🚌 23, 27, 41, 42

Filmhouse Café (£)

See page 58.

Henderson's at St John's (£)

See page 58.

Jacksons (££–£££)

In a basement off Royal Mile, very much aimed at tourists but none the worse for that, serving up Scottish specialities and a good selection of whiskies. Full of atmosphere.

✉ 209 High Street ☎ 0131 225 1793; www.jacksons-restaurant.co.uk
🕓 Daily 12–2:30, 5–10:30 🚌 23, 27, 35, 41, 42

Ondine (£££)

Opened at the end of 2009, this is a real oasis for seafood lovers. Celebrated Edinburgh-born chef Roy Brett sources only the freshest of local ingredients. Book a table or drop by to savour oysters at the chic bar, housed within the Missoni complex.

✉ 2 George IV Bridge ☎ 0131 226 1888; www.ondinerestaurant.co.uk
🕓 Tue–Sat 12–10, Sun 12–4 🚌 23, 27, 45

Petit Paris (££)

A popular Grassmarket restaurant with a friendly atmosphere serving a well-balanced range of authentic French cuisine in a straightforward manner. There are both traditional dishes and delicious crêpes; take your own wine if required.

✉ 38–40 Grassmarket ☎ 0131 226 2442; www.petitparis-restaurant.co.uk
🕓 Tue–Sun 12–3, 5:30–late 🚌 2, 35, 42

Le Sept (££–£££)

This attractive and lively bistro, tucked off Royal Mile, specializes in crêpes with a wide range of delicious fillings. Aberdeen Angus steaks and Scottish salmon also feature on the menu.

✉ 5 Hunter Square ☎ 0131 225 5428; www.eloc.demon.co.uk 🕓 Mon–Fri 12–2:15, 6–late, Sat 12–late, Sun 12:30–late 🚌 8, 29, 35

Tower Restaurant (£££)

The modern interior of this stylish restaurant above the Museum of Scotland, with superb views over Old Town to the castle, is a pleasant setting for dining out. A choice of eclectic dishes features on the menu.

✉ Museum of Scotland, Chambers Street ☎ 0131 225 3003; www.tower-restaurant.com 🕓 Daily 12–11 🚌 23, 27, 41, 42

Viva Mexico (££)

This well-established and popular Mexican restaurant offers a good choice of authentic spicy dishes, served in a relaxed and friendly atmosphere. Book the window table for a good view.

✉ 41 Cockburn Street ☎ 0131 226 5145; www.viva-mexico.co.uk
🕓 Mon–Sat 12–2, 6:30–10:30, Sun 6:30–10 🚌 3, 8, 33, 35, 36

The Witchery by the Castle (£££)

Two candlelit dining rooms close to the castle make up one of Edinburgh's best restaurants, where you can sample an interesting range of Scottish cuisine.

✉ 352 Castlehill ☎ 0131 225 5613; www.thewitchery.com 🕓 Daily 12–4, 5:30–11:30 🚌 23, 27, 41

SHOPPING

Anta

Everything is made in Scotland here. Take your pick from throws and cushions, fabrics and furniture. For gifts there is a range of stoneware and a choice of lovely tiles.

✉ Crockets's Land, 91–93 West Bow ☎ 0131 225 4616 🚌 2, 23, 27, 41

Iain Mellis Cheesemonger

A tiny wedge-shaped shop that specializes in perfectly conditioned cheese. Good sideline in organic foods – tasting is encouraged.

✉ 30a Victoria Street ☎ 0131 226 6215 🚌 23, 27, 35, 41, 42

Kinross Cashmere Store

A Royal Mile store selling sweaters, cardigans, scarves, dresses and skirts with a serious touch of luxury.

✉ 2 St Giles Street, Royal Mile ☎ 0131 225 5178 🚌 23, 35

Mr Wood's Fossils

A unique shop selling, and still unearthing, fossils of plants and animals. Founded in 1983, they first supplied museums but now specialize in retailing. Friendly and knowledgeable staff will fill you in on "Lizzie", the oldest reptile ever discovered.

✉ 5 Cowgatehead ☎ 0131 220 1344 🚌 2, 23, 27, 41, 42

Ness Scotland

A great place to track down take-home gifts, this Royal Mile shop sells 100 per cent Scottish lambswool accessories in the shape of gloves, mittens, scarves and bags in a multitude of colours.

✉ 367 High Street ☎ 0131 226 5227 🚍 23, 35, 41

Royal Mile Whiskies

This is one of Scotland's leading whisky specialists, focusing on single malts from all of Scotland's whisky-producing regions and rare grain whisky. Over 300 whiskies, and Havana cigars.

✉ 379 High Street, Royal Mile ☎ 0131 225 3383 🚍 23, 27, 35, 41, 42

ENTERTAINMENT

CINEMAS

Cameo

Small independent West End cinema specializing in new art-house releases, cult late-night movies and low-key Hollywood films.

✉ 38 Home Street ☎ 0131 228 2800 🚍 10, 11, 23, 27

Filmhouse

An independent cinema, showing an eclectic range of art-house and classic movies. Top-quality films from around the world.

✉ 88 Lothian Road ☎ 0131 228 2688; www.filmhousecinema.com
🚍 10, 11, 15, 34

CULTURAL VENUES

Edinburgh Festival Theatre

This international theatre offers ballet, drama, variety and dance, as well as all of Scottish Opera's Edinburgh performances.

✉ 13–29 Nicolson Street ☎ 0131 529 6000; www.eft.co.uk
🚍 3, 5, 7, 33, 37

Queens Hall

This converted church hosts a variety of concerts from modern and classical chamber music to jazz, folk, rock music and comedy.

✉ 89 Clerk Street ☎ 0131 668 2019; www.thequeenshall.net
🚍 3, 8, 29, 31, 37

Royal Lyceum Theatre Company

This magnificent Victorian theatre presents an integrated mix of classics and adaptations, with drama, tragedy, thrillers and comedy, as well as new works.

✉ Grindlay Street ☎ 0131 248 4848; www.lyceum.org.uk 🚌 10, 15, 17, 22

Traverse Theatre

Saltire Court is a state-of-the-art building completed in 1991. Home to the leading theatre company in Scotland which stages new and orginal productions.

✉ Cambridge Street ☎ 0131 228 1404; www.traverse.co.uk 🚌 10, 11, 22

Usher Hall

The city's leading concert venue is a fitting home for the Royal Scottish National Orchestra as well as a prestigious Festival arena.

✉ Lothian Road ☎ 0131 228 1155; www.usherhall.co.uk
🚌 10, 11, 15, 17, 22

MOTOR TOURS
Highland Experience Tours

Local tour company running minibus tours to attractions outside the city, like Rosslyn Chapel and St Andrews, as well as further afield to Loch Lomond, the Highlands and the famous Loch Ness.

✉ Loch Ness Discovery Centre, 1 Parliament Square, High Street ☎ 0131 226 1414; www.highlandexperience.com 🚌 23, 27, 45

NIGHTCLUBS AND PUBS
Bennet's Bar

An elaborate Victorian bar with authentic decor close to King's Theatre, ideal for drama fans and a perfect place to enjoy good food and a pleasant ambience; closed Sunday lunch.

✉ 8 Leven Street ☎ 0131 229 5143 🚌 10, 11, 23, 27

Ensign Ewart

Close to Edinburgh Castle, this popular pub, named after a hero of Waterloo, offers good food and beer. Regular folk music sessions.

✉ 521 Lawnmarket ☎ 0131 225 7440 🚌 23, 27, 35, 41

Espionage

Packed dance floors and four bars popular with locals, students and visitors. Commercial House, chart-toppers and eighties music.

✉ 9 Victoria Street ☎ 0131 477 7007 🚌 2, 23, 27, 35, 41

The Hive

Many of the nearby old Subway's club nights have moved to this venue, boasting a wide range of concerts with a definite bias towards alternative rock. Cheap drinks attract the student crowd.

✉ 15–17 Niddry Street ☎ 0131 556 0444 🚌 23, 27, 35

HMV Picture House

Edinburgh's newest live-music venue is a welcome addition, hosting many big names. Dance to the bands below or nip upstairs where comfortable seats await more sedentary souls.

✉ 31 Lothian Road ☎ 0131 221 2280; www.mamagroup.co.uk/picturehouse
🚌 1, 10, 15

WALKING TOURS

Edinburgh Literary Pub Tour

Professional actors take you through the streets, wynds and pubs associated with some of the great names in Scottish literature.

✉ 97b West Bow ☎ 0131 226 6665; www.edinburghliterarypubtour.co.uk
🚌 2

Mercat Walking Tours

A series of walks around hidden aspects of the Old Town, many starting from the Mercat Cross (► 87), includes subterranean passages and vaults, accompanied by historical commentaries.

✉ Mercat House, 28 Blair Street ☎ 0131 225 5445; www.mercattours.com
🚌 35

Saints and Sinners

Historical walking tours retracing the events that shaped Edinburgh, with plenty of quirky and macabre titbits thrown in.

✉ The Hub Festival Centre, Castlehill, Royal Mile ☎ 0131 07803 475688;
www.edinburghsaintsandsinners.co.uk

Canongate and Holyrood

Canongate forms the eastern end of the Royal Mile. It gets its name from the Augustine monks or "canons" who created a settlement close to the 12th-century Holyrood Abbey. Canongate was outside the walls of the city, relying on the sanctity of the abbey for protection.

Holyrood Park

The Canongate Tolbooth was the administrative headquarters of the borough until it became part of the city in 1856. This may not be the prettiest of Edinburgh's streets but it contains some of the best social history museums. At the bottom end of Canongate is the antithesis to these old buildings, the controversial and expensive Scottish Parliament Building. Behind this is another nod to modernity, the excellent Our Dynamic Earth science museum. The Royal Mile culminates in the splendid Palace of Holyroodhouse, the Queen's official residence in Scotland. Beyond is the huge open space of Holyrood Park with Arthur's Seat at its heart, a wonderful area to walk and relax in after sightseeing.

ARTHUR'S SEAT
Best places to see, ➤ 36–37.

HOLYROOD ABBEY
View the remains of Holyrood Abbey, founded in 1128 by David I, on a visit to the Palace of Holyroodhouse (➤ 48–49). Legend tells that the king was thrown from his horse by a huge stag; while grappling with it he found a crucifix in his hands and later dreamed that he should found a monastery of the Holy Rood, or Cross, on the site. The present abbey was built for the Augustinians in the early 13th century, a cathedral-sized structure with superb medieval facade. Burned by the English in 1544, partially destroyed after the Reformation, the Abbey was the scene of Charles I's coronation. In 1588 an Edinburgh mob desecrated the royal tombs, and in 1768 much of the remaining fabric collapsed.

✚ 12D ✉ The Palace of Holyroodhouse ☎ 0131 556 5100; www.royalcollection.org.uk ⏰ Apr–Oct daily 9:30–6; Nov–Mar 9:30–4:30. As the palace is a royal residence, opening times may be subject to change at short notice – telephone to check ✋ Expensive 🚌 35, 36

HOLYROOD PARK
Once a royal hunting preserve, Holyrood Park, which includes Arthur's Seat (➤ 36–37), is unique. No other European city has a piece of wild countryside, complete with three lochs, dramatic cliffs and moorland, a stone's throw of its heart. Queen's Drive, built at the request of Prince Albert, runs around the park and up towards Arthur's Seat; a pleasant drive, it's closed to all commercial vehicles. At its highest point is Dunsapie Loch, another of Albert's inspirations. Don't miss St Margaret's Well, a medieval Gothic structure near Holyrood Palace where a clear spring wells from beneath sculpted vaulting.

✚ 23J ✉ Holyrood Park ☎ 0131 652 8150 (Historic Scotland Ranger Service) ⏰ Open access, no vehicular access on Sun (except to Dunsapie Loch) ✋ Free 🚌 14, 21, 35, 44

JOHN KNOX HOUSE

Whether or not the key figure in Scotland's 16th-century Reformation actually died in the this building is open to debate, but the tradition was enough to prevent the destruction of this fine 1450 burgh house, with its overhanging gables and picturesque windows. Today, it houses an exhibition on the complex subject of the Scottish Reformation, complete with an audio re-enactment of Knox's famous audience with Mary, Queen of Scots, when he condemned the Mass and her love of dancing. You can also learn about the house's other famous inhabitant, James Mossman, the goldsmith who made the Scottish crown. He was probably responsible for the lovely carved frieze on the exterior that reads: LOVE. GOD. ABVFE. AL. AND. YI. NYCHTBOVR. AS. YI. SELF. The house is also home to The Scottish Storytelling Centre.

✠ 8D ✉ 43–45 High Street, Royal Mile ☎ 0131 556 9579
🕓 Mon–Sat 10–6; also Sun 12–6 during Edinburgh Festival
✋ Moderate 🍴 Cafe (£) 🚌 3, 7, 33, 35, 37

MUSEUM OF CHILDHOOD

The Museum of Childhood is a delight, its five galleries crammed with everything from train sets and tiddlywinks to teddies and tricycles. It started life in 1955 as the brainchild of town councillor Patrick Murray, who, right from the start, set his own distinctive mark on the vast range of exhibits – many

of the quirky and informative labels were written by him. Apart from the huge collection of toys from all over the world, many of them very old indeed, there are sections devoted to children's clothes, books, education, food and medicine. You can watch re-runs of old cartoons, listen to playground songs and children chanting multiplication tables and admire some truly palatial dolls' houses. The galleries echo with the cry "I remember that" as grandparents, parents and kids rediscover the joys of childhood.

www.cac.org.uk

✚ 8E ✉ 42 High Street, Royal Mile ☎ 0131 529 4142
🕐 Mon–Sat 10–5, Sun 12–5
🖐 Free 🚌 3, 7, 14, 33, 35

MUSEUM OF EDINBURGH

The three tenements comprising the Museum of Edinburgh, a warren of passages, crooked stairs and oddly shaped rooms, are as fascinating as the collections they house, which tell the history of Edinburgh. The building dates from 1570, and was home to merchants, aristocrats and working people at different times in its history; you can see how they lived in the room interiors scattered throughout. There's almost too much to see in one visit, with displays following Edinburgh's development from Roman times to the 19th century. The eclectic mix includes everything from silver to shop signs, but most visitors particularly enjoy the sight of Greyfriars Bobby's collar and bowl (➤ 84); while more serious-minded visitors shouldn't miss the 1638 National Covenant, signed by the Presbyterian leadership.

www.cac.org.uk

✚ 9D ✉ Huntley House, 142 Canongate, Royal Mile ☎ 0131 529 4143
🕐 Mon–Sat 10–5; also Sun 12–5 during Edinburgh Festival 🖐 Free
🚌 3, 7, 14, 33, 35

OUR DYNAMIC EARTH

Best places to see, ➤ 46–47.

PALACE OF HOLYROODHOUSE

Best places to see, ➤ 48–49.

THE PEOPLE'S STORY

For an insight into Edinburgh's social history pause on your way down the Royal Mile to visit The People's Story, a fascinating museum crammed with the minutiae of everyday life. There's a

wealth of objects and informative displays on everything from local bakers and brewers to tea rooms and pubs. The reconstructions of rooms provide a graphic illustration of the extent of Edinburgh's housing problems right into the 20th century.

www.cac.org.uk

✚ 9D ✉ Canongate Tolbooth, 163 Canongate, Royal Mile ☎ 0131 529 4057 ⏰ Mon–Sat 10–5; also Sun 12–5 during Edinburgh Festival ✋ Free

🚌 3, 7, 14, 33, 35

SCOTTISH PARLIAMENT BUILDING

Nearly 300 years after its last session, the Scottish Parliament opened once more in 1999, and has now found a permanent home at Holyrood. The architect, the late Enric Miralles, visualized the structure as "sitting in the land", and the design and surrounding landscape reflect this. Architecturally, the building is a stunner, and so it should be, with the cost topping £400 million. The main focus is the Debating Chamber, an airy wood-and-steel, light-filled space. Four tower buildings contain committee and meeting rooms, and offices. You can explore the whole complex, learn more at the visitor's exhibition or attend a debate in the public galleries. The best time to visit is on non-business days when the chamber and committee rooms are open to the public.
www.scottish.parliament.uk

➕ 11D ✉ Holyrood Road ☎ 0131 348 5200 🕐 Business days (normally Tue–Thu) 9–7; non-business days (usually Mon, Fri and weekdays when

Parliament is in recess) Apr–Oct 10–6; Nov–Mar 10–4 🖐 Free; guided tours: moderate 🍽 Cafe (£) 🚌 35, 41 ❓ Tours: Sat–Sun 10:20–2:40; Nov–Mar Mon–Fri 10:20–2:40; Apr–Oct Mon–Fri 10:20–4:40; duration 1 hour, book in advance

TRON KIRK

Christ's Kirk at the Tron, a fine Palladian-Gothic church built between 1637 and 1663, got its name from the salt-tron, a public weighbeam, which stood outside. In 1785, the south aisle was demolished to make room for the bridges linking the Old and New Towns. The church tower was destroyed by fire in 1824, and replaced in 1828. Closed for worship since 1952, the Tron Kirk housed the Old Town Information Centre until 2006, but is at present closed awaiting its future.

✚ 7E ✉ 122 High Street, Royal Mile 🕐 View from the outside only
🚌 3, 5, 14, 31, 35

HOTELS

Bank (££)

This small, distinctive and privately owned hotel in one of Royal Mile's landmark buildings offers a memorable Scottish experience. It benefited from refurbishment in 2008.

✉ 1 South Bridge ☎ 0131 556 9940; www.festival-inns.co.uk
🚌 3, 18, 14, 35

Jury's Inn (££)

The modern chain hotel, close to Waverley Station and the Royal Mile, offers bright, cheerful and spacious rooms.

✉ 43 Jeffrey Street ☎ 0131 200 3300/0400; www.jurysdoyle.com 🚌 36

Macdonald Holyrood Hotel (££)

Situated next to the Scottish Parliament Building, the Macdonald offers a good level of accommodation with comfortable rooms and facilities, including an award-winning restaurant and a heated pool.

✉ 81 Holyrood Road ☎ 0870 194 2106; www.macdonaldhotels.co.uk 🚌 36

Royal Mile Backpackers (£)

Only a short walk from Waverley Station and all the major sights, this hostel is small and cosy with a self-catering kitchen.

✉ 105 High Street ☎ 0131 557 6120; www.royalmilebackpackers.com
🚌 35, 36

RESTAURANTS

Ayutthaya (££)

Warm and relaxed restaurant opposite the Festival Theatre offering an extensive and varied range of authentic Thai dishes; book if you're eating before the theatre.

✉ 14b Nicolson Street ☎ 0131 556 9351; www.ayutthayaedinburgh.co.uk
🕓 Daily 12–3, 5:30–11 🚌 7, 8, 14, 33

David Bann (£–££)

Considered to be the city's best vegetarian restaurant, this great choice offers imaginative dishes in slick, minimalist surroundings. There is an international flavour to the menu, which offers snacks, full meals, salads and side dishes and a tempting selection of desserts.

✉ 56–58 St Mary Street ☎ 0131 556 5888; www.davidbann.com ⏰ Daily 11am–late 🚌 7, 8, 14, 35, 36

Dubh Prais (££)

An intimate whitewashed cellar houses one of the Royal Mile's better bets, where you'll find traditional Scottish cuisine using local ingredients such as venison and salmon, backed up by delicious desserts and a fine range of whiskies.

✉ 123b High Street ☎ 0131 557 5732; www.dubhpraisrestaurant.com ⏰ Tue–Sat 5–10:30pm 🚌 23, 27, 35, 41

Kalpna (£–££)

This well-established Southside Indian restaurant serves a wide range of vegetarian dishes, subtly blending fresh spices into authentic Gujarati flavours.

✉ 2–3 St Patrick's Square ☎ 0131 667 9890; www.kalpnarestaurant.com ⏰ Mon–Sat 12–2, 5:30–10:30, Sun only during Festival 🚌 7, 8, 14, 33

Off the Wall (££–£££)

David Anderson's fine restaurant is based in the French tradition, but uses only the best of Scottish produce in his dishes. The set-price lunch menu is good value and the dinner menu delights with such dishes as saddle of venison and seared salmon.

✉ 105 High Street, Royal Mile ☎ 0131 558 1497 ⏰ Mon–Sat 12–2, 7–10 🚌 23, 27, 35

Pancho Villas (££)

This lively Mexican restaurant is a very popular party venue, located in the Royal Mile. It offers authentic national dishes and an excellent choice of vegetarian meals, all of which are made with the best seasonal ingredients and locally sourced produce. Be sure to try one of their margaritas.

✉ 240 Canongate ☎ 0131 557 4416; www.panchovillas.co.uk ⏰ Mon–Thu 12–2:30, 6–10:30, Fri 12–10:30, Sat 12–11, Sun 6–10:30 (summer 12–10:30); Jul, Aug daily 12–11 🚌 35

Wedgwood the Restaurant (££)

A breath of fresh air among the glut of tourist orientated restaurants in this part of town. Fresh Scottish ingredients are married with culinary influences from all over in a winning mix.

✉ 267 Canongate ☎ 0131 558 8737; www.wedgwoodtherestaurant.co.uk
🕐 Mon–Sat 12–3, 6–10, Sun 12:30–3:30, 6–10 🚌 35, 36

Wee Windaes (££)

See page 59.

SHOPPING

Bagpipes Galore

Everything to do with bagpipes, plus accessories and CDs.

✉ 82 Canongate ☎ 031 556 4073; www.bagpipe.co.uk 🚌 35

Blackwells

Formerly James Thin, this shop has been providing general and academic books and publications for more than 150 years.

✉ 53–62 South Bridge ☎ 0131 622 8222; www.blackwells.com
🚌 3, 5, 8, 14, 29

Designs on Cashmere

Cashmere is not a cheap option, but the quality and pure luxury is never in question.

✉ 28 High Street ☎ 0131 556 6394 🚌 35

ENTERTAINMENT

Bongo Club

This cafe and exhibition area offers hip club and live music nights. Local and international underground acts appear here.

✉ Moray House, 37 Holyrood Road ☎ 0131 558 7604;
www.thebongoclub.co.uk 🚌 35

Whistle Binkies

Centrally located, providing live music seven nights a week and open until the small hours – an excellent place to enjoy a drink.

✉ 4–6 South Bridge ☎ 0131 557 5114; www.whistlebinkies.com
🚌 3, 7, 8, 14, 29

New Town

When overcrowding in the Old Town reached crisis point in the mid-18th century, the great and the good of Edinburgh needed a solution. As a result of a competition to find the perfect "new" town, the superb and elegant area of New Town was born. This was a far cry from the dark and dirty alleys and crowded tenements down by the castle. Space, grandeur and elegance were the order of the day.

One of the most remarkable observations about the city is how the Old and New towns sit side by side and yet are so incomparably diverse. Most visitors head straight for the castle and the Royal Mile but many stay in the New Town, with its town house hotels and pretty squares. The restaurants, bars and cafes of the streets behind the main thoroughfare, Princes Street, are buzzing both day and night. A walk farther out will give breathing space and peace, a welcome break from the busy city centre.

ASSEMBLY ROOMS

Even if you're not attending a concert, the Assembly Rooms, opened in 1787, are well worth a quick visit. The plain facade, with its massive 1818 portico, leads to a series of elegantly proportioned rooms planned for equally elegant social occasions. The ballroom, 28m (31yds) by more than 13m (14yds), is lit by chandeliers; the music hall, even larger, is equally impressive. The Assembly Rooms are a key Festival venue.

www.assemblyroomsedinburgh.co.uk

🕂 4C ✉ 54 George Street ☎ 0131 220 4348 ❸ Check beforehand that the rooms have not been hired for a function ✋ Varies for performances
🚌 24, 29, 42

CALTON HILL

A clutch of remarkable monuments adorns the slopes of Calton Hill (108m/354ft), another remnant of the volcano that formed Edinburgh's geological structure. The view from the hill's summit is splendid, with all Edinburgh spreading around, and vistas down the coast and across to Fife. For even wider views, climb the 143 steps to the top of **Nelson Monument,** built in 1807, and housing a timepiece in the shape of a white ball which drops from a mast each day at 1pm. Next to it looms the unfinished National Monument; modelled on the Parthenon in Athens, it was intended as a memorial to the Scots who fell in the Napoleonic Wars. Only 12 columns had been completed when the money ran out and it was known for years as "Edinburgh's Disgrace". The City Observatory, with its Gothic tower and astronomical dome, stands nearby; the grandiose Playfair Monument commemorates John Playfair, first president of the Astronomical Institution.

www.cac.org.uk

🕂 9B ✉ Calton Hill 🚌 5, 45

Nelson Monument

✉ Calton Hill ☎ 0131 529 3993 ❸ Apr–Sep Mon 1–6, Tue–Sat 10–6; Oct–Mar Mon–Sat 10–3 ✋ Moderate 🚌 5, 26, 33, 45

CHARLOTTE SQUARE

Charlotte Square, named after Queen
Charlotte, wife of George III, was designed by
Robert Adam in 1791 as part of the first New
Town (▶ 44–45). This triumphant and
harmonious example of symmetrical
architecture, with its central garden, was
planned to balance St Andrew Square at the
other end of George Street. The north and
south sides of the square present an unbroken
facade which hides the blocks' 11 individual
houses. The west side is occupied by West
Register House, originally St George's Church,
an impressive porticoed building topped by a
cupola. The square was intended for
residential use, though today many of the
buildings house offices. For a glimpse of
18th-century life head for the Georgian House
(▶ 118–119) on the north side.

🚆 2D ✉ Charlotte Square 🍴 Restaurants, bars and
cafes on George Street (£–££) 🚌 12, 19, 36, 37, 41

CITY ART CENTRE

The City Art Centre was established in 1980 in a building originally constructed in 1899, a splendid baroque edifice with an imaginatively converted interior. Its six galleries house the city's collection of Scottish art and provide space for a diverse range of temporary exhibitions – you're as likely to find a show devoted to *Star Wars* as to Michelangelo drawings or Egyptian antiquities. The permanent collection includes paintings, watercolours, photographs and sculpture. Look for works by William MacTaggart, J P Fergusson and Anne Redpath, all important 20th-century Edinburgh artists and members of the school known as the Scottish Colourists.

www.cac.org.uk

✚ 7D ✉ 2 Market Street ☎ 0131 529 3993 ⏰ Mon–Sat 10–5, Sun 12–5 💷 Free, but charge for entrance to major temporary exhibitions 🍴 Licensed cafe (£–££) 🚌 3, 3A, 31, 33, 36

GEORGE STREET

The central street of the three that form the grid of the first stage of the 1766 New Town, George Street has escaped the development that damaged some of the architecture of Princes Street (➤ 121). This spacious thoroughfare, designed by James Craig and named after George III, is still liberally endowed with Georgian buildings, many of them housing prestigious businesses and smart shops. St Andrew's Church (1785), with its fine Corinthian portico, stands near the east end; it was here, in 1843, that dissenting ministers walked out of the General Assembly to found the Free Church of Scotland. Farther west, the Assembly Rooms (1787; ➤ 114) are worth a visit, while several of the opulent Victorian edifices which once housed banks have been transformed into elegant and lively wine bars, popular with Edinburgh's young professionals.

✚ 2D–5C ✉ George Street 🍴 The Living Room (£–££; ➤ 132) 🚌 24, 29, 42

GEORGIAN HOUSE

The Georgian House, on the north side of Robert Adam's Charlotte Square, offers a chance to see how Edinburgh's monied classes lived in the grand houses of the New Town. Reconstruction of the interior involved restoring the original decoration scheme, weaving fabrics for curtains and coverings, and tracking down furniture, rugs, paintings and fittings. You can see the ground-floor dining room, laid up with Wedgwood and silver, and, in true 18th-century style, a ground-floor bedroom, with a smart four-poster bed. The fashionably sparsely furnished drawing room runs the full width of the house upstairs, while the basement kitchen was the height of convenience in Georgian times. It's crammed with utensils and dominated by the huge range. Note the blue walls; it was believed that blue kept the flies away.

www.nts.org.uk

➕ 2C ✉ 7 Charlotte Square ☎ 0131 226 3318 🕒 Mar daily 11–4; Apr–Jun, Sep, Oct 10–5; Jul–Aug 10–6; Nov 11–3; closed Dec–Feb 🖐 Moderate, but free to National Trust and National Trust for Scotland members 🍴 Restaurant on site (£) 🚌 3, 12, 19, 36, 37, 41

HANOVER STREET

For one of the best views to be had in New Town, walk in either direction up and down the slopes of Hanover Street, the easternmost of the three streets crossing the grid pattern of the First New Town. To the south is the Classical facade of the Royal Scottish Academy, with the Mound, Assembly Hall and New College rising behind. To the north, the slopes drop away to give far views to the Firth of Forth and the Fife hills. The statue at the junction with George Street shows George IV, seemingly enjoying much the same vista.

✚ 5C–5D ✉ Hanover Street 🍴 Henderson's Salad Table (£; ➤ 132) 🚌 13, 23, 27, 28

THE MOUND

Until the 1760s the site now occupied by Princes Street Gardens was filled with an unlovely lake known as the Nor' Loch, created as a northern defence for the castle in 1460. In 1763 it was partially drained for

the construction of the North Bridge, to allow access to the planned New Town. To the west the marshy ground was gradually bridged by the mounds of earth from the building works to the north; by 1784 it was a rough causeway for carriages and was completed by 1830. An estimated two million cartloads of dumped earth went into its construction – a veritable mound. Its two landmarks are the Royal Scottish Academy (➤ 123) and the National Gallery of Scotland (➤ 42–43).

✚ 5D ✉ The Mound 🚌 23, 27, 41, 42

NATIONAL GALLERY OF SCOTLAND

Best places to see, ➤ 42–43.

NEW TOWN
Best places to see, ➤ 45–46.

PRINCES MALL (WAVERLEY MARKET)
Waverley Market, renamed Princes Mall, opened in 1984 and occupies the site of the old vegetable market, which was displaced in the 19th century by a market hall used for concerts and exhibitions. This familiar landmark was demolished to make way for today's functional granite structure, whose flat roof, level with Princes Street, houses Edinburgh's main tourist office. The speciality shopping mall, with more than 40 shops, is a good place to hunt for unusual clothes and gifts. There's a convenient fast food area and a rooftop cafe, for a quick lunch in between sightseeing.
www.princesmall-edinburgh.co.uk

✚ 6C ✉ Princes Street East End ☎ 0131 557 3759 ⊙ Mon–Wed, Fri, Sat 8:30–6, Thu 8:30–7; Sun 11–5 🚌 3, 8, 10, 17, 25, 27, 29

PRINCES STREET

Its situation alone makes Princes Street one of Europe's great thoroughfares, a straight and stately division between the Old Town and the New, with views south across Princes Street Gardens to the fabulous silhouette of the castle and Royal Mile. Lined with department and high street stores, Princes Street is where Edinburgh folk come to shop, and its streets are full of shoppers throughout the day. Built from 1769, it was named after George III's two sons. Princes Street once presented the stylish and harmonious face of restrained Georgian architecture, but deteriorated in the 19th and 20th centuries when dignified buildings were replaced with some architectural disasters. Currently these are being replaced with elegant shopping and residential complexes, restoring some much-needed style to this superbly sited street.

🚻 3D–7C ⊠ Princes Street 🍴 Henderson's at St John's (£; ➤ 58)
🚌 3, 10, 17, 25, 44 and many others

PRINCES STREET GARDENS

The green oasis of Princes Street Gardens occupies the site of the old Nor' Loch (➤ 119), drained during the construction of the New Town. The 8ha (20-acre) West Gardens, laid out in 1816–20 for the Princes Street inhabitants, are separated from the 3ha (7.5-acre) East Garden by the Royal Scottish Academy (➤ 123); both gardens became a much-loved public park in 1876. They are laid out conventionally and attractively with specimen trees, sweeping lawns and riotously bright planting. Children will love the Floral Clock in the West Garden, planted every year on a different theme; watch out for the cuckoo when the hour strikes. The gardens are edged with statues, which include the explorer David Livingstone, and James Young Simpson, the pioneer of the safe use of chloroform.

✚ 4D ✉ Princes Street 🍴 Snack bars and kiosks in gardens (£)
🚌 3, 10, 17, 25, 44 and many others

QUEEN STREET

Queen Street runs parallel with Princes Street (➤ 121) and George Street (➤ 117), a long stretch of fine Georgian architecture largely untouched by modern development. The street, built between 1769 and 1792, was named after Queen Charlotte, wife of George III. Most of its buildings now house offices, but the fine views towards the Firth of Forth remain unchanged, as do the private gardens along the north side. James Young Simpson, the pioneer of anaesthesia, conducted his experiments on himself inside No 52.

✚ 2C–6B ✉ Queen Street 🚌 8, 23, 27, 42

ROYAL SCOTTISH ACADEMY

This lovely Classical building, designed by William Playfair in 1822,

is a fitting home for Scotland's Royal Academy, which moved here permanently in 1910. The Academy, founded in 1826, is based loosely on London's Royal Academy, and has both Academicians and Associates. It is at the forefront of art promotion in Scotland and to this end holds two major exhibitions annually; the Students' Art Exhibition and the Annual Exhibition. The Academy also lets the building to other arts organizations, such as the Royal Scottish Society of Painters in Watercolour and the Society of Scottish Artists, who stage their shows in the spacious galleries. It is also an important Festival exhibition venue, when its steps are thronged with Festival-goers enjoying street performances in the square outside.

www.royalscottishacademy.org

✚ 5D ✉ The Mound ☎ 0131 225 6671 🕐 Fri–Wed 10–5, Thu 10–7
✋ Varies according to exhibition 🚌 3, 23, 27, 41, 42

a walk around the New Town and Princes Street

Walk down North Charlotte Street and cross Queen Street to continue down Forres Street to Moray Place. Turn right and exit into Darnaway Street and along to Heriot Row. Continue along Heriot Row and cross the top of Howe Street to look at No 17 Heriot Row.

As you walk along Heriot Row, Queen Street Gardens are on your right; these were part of New Town's original plan to give householders access to green space. Number 17 Heriot Row was the childhood home of author Robert Louis Stevenson; look out for the plaque beside the front door.

Retrace your steps to turn right down Howe Street, then turn right again on to Northumberland Street. Where it meets Dundas Street turn right uphill, crossing Heriot Row and Queen Street to continue uphill on Hanover Street. Take the first right into Thistle Street and walk along to Frederick Street.

Thistle Street is one of the New Town's hidden and seductive shopping streets, where you'll find antique jewellers, elegant clothes shops and attractive cafes.

Turn left uphill, cross George Street and continue down to Princes Street. Turn left and cross the road.

You could take this opportunity to climb the Scott Monument (➤ 54–55) or visit the Royal Scottish Academy (➤ 123) or the National Gallery of Scotland (➤ 42–43), which stands just behind it.

With your back to the castle turn left along Princes Street or walk through Princes Street Gardens (➤ 122). At the end of the gardens, cross Princes Street and go straight ahead up South Charlotte Street.

Distance 4km (2.5 miles)
Time 1.5 hours walking; 4 hours with stops for visits
Start/end point Charlotte Square
✚ 2D 🚌 3, 12, 19, 36, 37, 41
Lunch Urbanangel (£) ✉ 121 Hanover Street ☎ 0131 225 6215

ST ANDREW SQUARE

Edinburgh's financial heart, St Andrew Square, lies
at the east end of George Street, and acts as the
architectural counterbalance to Charlotte Square at
the west end. Its design, dating from 1767, is not as
instantly pleasing. The grandiose mansion on the
east side, built in 1772 for Sir Laurence Dundas,
now houses the headquarters of the Royal Bank of
Scotland; another Dundas, Henry, 1st Earl of
Melville, surveys much of the New Town from the
central column. On the northeast side is Multrees
Walk, a prestigious shopping mall fronted by Harvey
Nichols' stylish department store.

🕇 6C ✉ St Andrew Square 🍽 Forth Floor Restaurant at
Harvey Nichols (££; ➤ 131) 🚌 8, 12, 17, 26, 29

SCOTT MONUMENT

Best places to see, ➤ 54–55.

SCOTTISH NATIONAL PORTRAIT GALLERY

The imposing red sandstone bulk of the Scottish
National Portrait Gallery looms over the east end of
Queen Street. Built in the 1880s, it's worth a visit for
the interior alone, with its wonderful arcaded
entrance hall glittering with lustrous murals. The
entire collection is devoted to the Scots, though
not all the portraits are by Scots. You can trace the
flow of Scottish history and achievement through
this diverse collection, though most people head
straight for Mary, Queen of Scots, Alexander
Nasmyth's portrait of Robert Burns and Henry
Raeburn's portrait of Sir Walter Scott. Modern
Scots to look for include Jean Muir, the fashion
designer, the actor Sean Connery and Irvine Welsh,

the author of *Trainspotting*. The gallery closed in 2009 to let work start on the *Portrait of the Nation* project, which will see improved facilities and displays. It is scheduled to re-open in the autumn of 2011.

www.nationalgalleries.org

✚ 6B ✉ 1 Queen Street ☎ 0131 624 6200; 🕓 Fri–Wed 10–5, Thu 10–7 ♿ Free 🍴 Queen Street Café (£–££)
🚌 8, 10, 12, 16, 23, 27 ❓ Charges for special exhibitions

WATERLOO PLACE

Waterloo Place is the continuation of Princes Street to the east, a superbly balanced example of grandiose neoclassical architectural design. If you're hurrying through on your way to Calton Hill, pause to admire the soaring facades of its buildings. Waterloo Place runs through the Old Calton cemetery; here are buried some of the major figures of the Scottish Enlightenment such as the philosopher David Hume, and there's a fine view back to the castle. More prosaically, the bottom of the place gives access to the St James Centre, a hideous blocklike concrete structure housing a wide range of shops. The public outcry following its construction probably did more than anything else to further the cause of Edinburgh's conservation during the early 1970s.

Scenes from the cult film *Trainspotting* (1995) were shot in Edinburgh, where the action is set, though most locations are in Glasgow. Look out for Pivo Caffe near Waterloo Place; this is where Renton runs into a car in the opening scene.

✚ 7–8C ✉ Waterloo Place 🍴 Bars and cafes (£)
🚌 7, 8, 14, 22, 29

HOTELS

Ailsa Craig (£)
Enjoy the Georgian splendours of the tree-lined Royal Terrace at this comfortable, reasonably priced hotel, only 10 minutes' walk from Waverley Station. Most rooms have views across the gardens to the Firth of Forth.

✉ 24 Royal Terrace ☎ 0131 556 1022; www.ailsacraighotel.co.uk
🚌 1, 5, 26

Balmoral (£££)
Dominating the east end of Princes Street with views of the city and castle and offering superb accommodation, a Michelin-star restaurant (number one, ➤ 133), an informal brasserie, bars, a pool, sauna and steam room, and superb service.

✉ 1 Princes Street ☎ 0131 556 2414; www.thebalmoralhotel.com
🚌 3, 8, 22, 29

Caledonian Hilton (£££)
Edinburgh's most famous hotel stands at the west end of Princes Street. The elegance of its interior lives up to its ornate exterior, with the comfort and service associated with a 5-star hotel.

✉ Princes Street ☎ 0131 222 8888; www.hilton.co.uk/caledonian
🚌 11, 15, 17

The Clarendon Hotel (££)
This refurbished hotel near the west end of Princes Street provides a comfortable base right in the city centre.

✉ 25 Shandwick Place ☎ 0131 229 1467; www.clarendonhoteledi.co.uk
🚌 12, 25, 26, 33

Dene Guest House (£)
You get a good breakfast to start your day at this friendly three-storey Georgian guesthouse at the north end of New Town. It's easy to get a bus up to the city centre or it's just a 10-minute walk away. There are eleven rooms, five have en-suite facilities and six share bathrooms.

✉ 7 Eyre Place ☎ 0131 556 2700; www.deneguesthouse.com 🚌 23, 27, 36

Howard (£££)

The sublime Howard, formed from three connected 18th-century houses, has lovely rooms, elegant public areas and an outstanding restaurant serving traditional Scottish fare. Close to the shops and major attractions. Secure, free car park and butler service.

✉ 34 Great King Street ☎ 0131 557 3500; www.thehoward.com 🚌 13

Macdonald Holyrood Hotel (££)

Built to tie in with the opening of the new Scottish Parliament building this four-star business hotel also works well for leisure guests, with a swimming pool, a decent restaurant and many rooms offering views of the parliament and out over Arthur's Seat. The buffet breakfasts are enough to keep you going all day.

✉ 81 Holyrood Road ☎ 0131 550 4500; www.macdonaldhotels.co.uk
🚌 35, 36

The Roxburghe (£££)

This refurbished hotel enjoys a perfect location at the west end of George Street. Chic rooms, a classy restaurant and a spa with a swimming pool complete a compelling cocktail.

✉ 38 Charlotte Square ☎ 0844 879 9063; www.macdonaldhotels.co.uk
🚌 3, 22, 29

The Rutland (££)

Revamped modern hotel at the end of Princes Street. Some rooms offer views of Princes Street and the castle, while all are stylish and well designed. The restaurant is worth a visit.

✉ 1–3 Rutland Street ☎ 0131 229 3402; www.therutlandhotel.com
🚌 3, 8, 22, 29

Tigerlily (££)

The best of the new boutique hotels that have opened in Edinburgh in recent years and a deserved award winner. One of George Street's most popular bars with an excellent restaurant and 33 idiosyncratic rooms with a real design element.

✉ 125 George Street ☎ 0131 225 5005; www.tigerlilyedinburgh.co.uk
🚌 3, 8, 22, 29

RESTAURANTS

Bar Roma (£)

Popular West End Italian restaurant that has for years served tasty pasta and pizza in generous portions in a happy relaxed atmosphere. Great for parties.

✉ 39a Queensferry Street ☎ 0131 225 2977; www.bar-roma.co.uk
🕓 Mon–Thu, Sun 12–12, Fri–Sat 12pm–1am 🚌 19, 36, 37, 41

Café Marlayne (£)

An excellent small French bistro that has quickly established a high reputation for its delicious food. It's best to reserve as space is limited, but it's well worth a visit.

✉ 76 Thistle Street ☎ 0131 226 2230; www.cafemarlayne.co.uk
🕓 Tue–Sat 12–2, 6–10 (also Mon in summer) 🚌 23, 29, 41

Café Royal Oyster Bar (£££)

The ornate Victorian design of this famous New Town institution provides the ideal setting in which to consume oysters, fish, seafood, Scottish game and vegetarian dishes.

✉ 19 West Register Street ☎ 0131 556 1884; www.caferoyal.org.uk
🕓 Daily 12–2, 6–9 🚌 8, 25, 29, 37

Café St Honoré (££)

With a fine blend of Scottish and French influences, this small friendly restaurant, tucked away in a quiet lane, offers imaginative dishes with Continental flair in an intimate atmosphere. A set menu is available between 5 and 7pm.

✉ 34 Thistle Street Lane ☎ 0131 226 2211; www.cafesthonore.com
🕓 Mon–Sat 12–2:15, 5–10 🚌 23, 29, 41

Centotre (££)

Swish, award-winning Italian restaurant set in a grand historic building that impresses both on the plate and with its surrounds. Buzzing atmosphere and freshly cooked pasta dishes. It's impossible to get a table during the Festival unless you book ahead.

✉ 103 George Street ☎ 0131 225; www.centotre.com 🕓 Mon–Thu 7:30am–10pm, Fri–Sat 7:30am–10:30pm, Sun 11–5 🚌 3, 8, 22, 29

Cuisine d'Odile (£)

A little piece of France in the pleasant basement of the Institut Français, offering superb, imaginative cuisine using local and seasonal ingredients. You can bring your own wine, if desired.

✉ 13 Randolph Crescent ☎ 0131 225 5685 🕐 Tue–Sat 12–2pm
🚌 19, 36, 37

Dome (£££)

Housed in a former bank, crowned by an impressive glass ceiling, the Grill Room has retained the original fittings. It serves classic Scottish cuisine blended with Eastern and European flavours.

✉ 14 George Street ☎ 0131 624 8624; www.thedomeedinburgh.com
🕐 Daily 12–late 🚌 13, 29, 42

Forth Floor Restaurant at Harvey Nichols (££)

Fine views of the Edinburgh skyline and excellent menus at this icon of international style, which opened in 2002. The great wine list, to suit every pocket, has been chosen to fit with the modern British cooking with a Scottish twist.

✉ 30–34 St Andrew Square ☎ 0131 524 8350; www.harveynichols.com
🕐 Mon–Fri 12–3, Sat–Sun 12–3:30, Tue–Sat 6–10 🚌 8, 10, 12, 29

Gusto (££)

The name may have changed from Est Est Est, but the bright modern interior and palate-tingling modern Mediterranean cooking remain. The set lunch menus offer excellent value for money in this expensive part of town.

✉ 135 George Street ☎ 0131 225 2555; www.gustorestaurants.uk.com
🕐 Daily 11–11 🚌 13, 19, 37, 41

Henderson's Salad Table (£)

This long-established vegetarian restaurant is an Edinburgh institution. Consistently good salads, soups, hot dishes and puddings and a friendly, lively atmosphere; be prepared to queue at busy times. Occasional live music.

✉ 94 Hanover Street ☎ 0131 225 2131; www.hendersonsofedinburgh.co.uk
🕐 Mon–Sat 8am–10:45pm (Sun during Festival) 🚌 23, 27, 41, 42

Indian Cavalry Club (££)

This classy Indian restaurant in the West End serves an outstanding range of authentic dishes.

✉ 22 Coates Crescent ☎ 0131 220 0138; www.indiancavalryclub.co.uk
🕐 Daily 12–2, 5–10:45 🚌 3, 12, 25, 26

Kay's Bar (£)

See page 58.

Kweilin (££)

A relaxed and popular restaurant serving the highest-quality Cantonese cuisine. Reservation recommended.

✉ 19–21 Dundas Street ☎ 0131 557 1875 🕐 Tue–Sat 12–2, 5–11, Sun 5–11 🚌 23, 27

The Living Room (£–££)

You'll find nothing fancy or fiddly, just quality ingredients and robust cooking. You can listen to jazz music on most nights. The large bar area makes it a good place for a pre-dinner drink.

✉ 113–115 George Street ☎ 0131 226 0880; www.thelivingroom.co.uk
🕐 Mon–Sat 11am–1am, Sun 11am–12:30am 🚌 13, 19, 37, 41 ❓ Usually jazz Tue–Sun

Mussel Inn (££)

Shellfish and other seafoods, all from sustainable and local sources, are served at this informal bistro-style restaurant in the heart of New Town, in both traditional and contemporary dishes.

✉ 61–65 Rose Street ☎ 0131 225 5979; www.mussel-inn.com 🕐 Mon–Thu 12–3, 6–10, Fri, Sat 12–10, Sun 12:30–10 🚌 3, 12, 29, 44

New Edinburgh Rendezvous (££)

Edinburgh's longest-established Chinese restaurant is still providing Beijing cuisine to a high standard in the West End; it also offers an imaginative selection of set menus.

✉ 10a Queensferry Street ☎ 0131 225 2023;
www.edinburghrendezvous.co.uk 🕐 Mon–Sat 12–2, 5:30–11, Sun 1–11
🚌 19, 37, 41

New York Steam Packet (£)

Themed on a ship's cabin, with stripped wooden floors and dimmed lights, this inconspicuous restaurant offers steaks, burgers, fish and vegetarian dishes cooked to order; you can bring your own wine or beer, if required. Service is cheerful and efficient.

✉ 31 Rose Street, North Lane ☎ 0131 220 4825; www.newyorksteampacket.co.uk 🕐 Daily 6–11 🚌 23, 29, 42

number one (£££)

This classy restaurant with its one Michelin star in the Balmoral Hotel (➤ 128) offers luxury cooking at luxury prices. Rich red walls displaying colourful prints, and large, well-spaced tables and gold velvet chairs provide the setting for a romantic meal and some seriously creative cuisine featuring the best of Scottish produce.

✉ 1 Princes Street ☎ 0131 557 6727; www.restaurantnumberone.com/restaurant 🕐 Daily 6:30–10pm 🚌 3, 8, 22, 29

Olive Branch (£–££)

The Olive Branch is an inviting place to sit back and watch the world go by through the big windows. This restaurant is perfect for a hearty late breakfast, a coffee stop, a chatty lunch or an intimate dinner. Brunch is very popular at the weekends.

✉ 91 Broughton Street ☎ 0131 557 8589; www.theolivebranchscotland.co.uk 🕐 Daily 10am–late 🚌 8, 17

Ruan Siam (££)

This lively, popular Thai restaurant in a small cellar serves a range of authentic aromatic delicacies, using the freshest ingredients; reservation recommended. There is a second branch, Ruan Thai at 29 Cockburn Street.

✉ 48 Howe Street ☎ 0131 226 3675; www.ruanthai.co.uk 🕐 Daily 12–2:30, 5:30–10:45 🚌 29

The Rutland (££)

See page 59.

Saigon Saigon (£)

Great all-day Chinese self-service buffet restaurant offering cheap, cheerful, basic Chinese dishes in well-designed canteen-style surroundings. Superb value.

✉ 15 South St Andrew Street ☎ 0131 557 3737 🕐 Daily 12–10:30
🚌 8, 12, 17

Stac Polly (££)

This restaurant, with its stone walls and tartan decoration, serves modern Scottish dishes in a relaxed atomosphere. There is a good selection of whiskies to round off your meal. There are sister restaurants at 8–10 Grindlay Street and 3–8 St Mary's Street.

✉ 29–33 Dublin Street ☎ 0131 556 2231; www.stacpolly.com 🕐 Mon–Fri 12–2:30, 6–11; Sat–Sun 6–11pm 🚌 8, 10, 11, 12, 16

Tampopo (££)

This tiny Japanese noodle bar specializes in takeouts, but has a few seats for eating in. Delicacies ranging from sushi to exquisite *bento* meals make it Edinburgh's finest Japanese establishment.

✉ 25a Thistle Street ☎ 0131 220 5254 🕐 Mon 12–3, Tue–Sat 12–3, 6–9
🚌 23, 24, 29, 42

Tigerlily (££)

The chic restaurant in the Tigerlily hotel (➤ 129) has an equally bright and inventive menu, which features a good choice of seafood dishes and there is also a main special of the day. Lobster and chips is a popular choice among decadent diners.

✉ 125 George Street ☎ 0131 225 5005; www.tigerlilyedinburgh.co.uk
🕐 Daily 8am–10:30pm 🚌 3, 8, 22, 29

Valvona and Crolla (££)

See page 59.

VinCaffé (£–£££)

Launched in 2004 to celebrate Valvona and Crolla's 70th anniversary, this stylish space, on Multrees Walk next to St Andrew's Square, offers excellent Italian food and wine with takeout hot drinks and snacks on the ground floor, and fine dining accompanied by even finer wines in the first-floor restaurant. It's just a 10-minute walk from Valvona and Crolla (► 59).

✉ Multrees Walk ☎ 0131 557 0088; www.valvonacrolla.co.uk 🕐 Cafe: Mon–Sat 8–late, Sun 11–5:30; restaurant: Mon–Fri 10am–late, Sat 9am–late, Sun 11am–5:30 🚌 8, 17, 26, 45

Wok & Wine (££)

Top-notch Chinese dining in a grand old Georgian-era stone building. Book a window table and take in the street action as you tuck into specialities from all regions of China. Good-value set meals and crisp Chinese beers complete a compelling experience at one of the city's best ethnic eateries.

✉ 57a Frederick Street ☎ 0131 225 2382; www.wokandwine.com 🕐 Daily 5:30–11pm 🚌 24, 29, 42

SHOPPING

CLOTHING AND WOOLLENS

Belinda Robertson

Belinda Robertson OBE is Scotland's foremost guru of the cashmere world, a knitwear designer with an international reputation for co-ordinating colour, design and the finest cashmere.

✉ 13 Dundas Street ☎ 0131 557 8118; www.belindarobertson.com 🚌 13, 23, 27

Dickson & MacNaughton

A long-established store stocking high-quality country clothing by all the leading manufacturers. The showrooms also display a full range of fishing and shooting accessories, including shooting sticks, field sport books, binoculars and much more.

✉ 21 Frederick Street ☎ 0131 225 4218; www.dicksonandmacnaughton.com 🚌 24, 29, 41, 42

Helen Bateman

This individual store carries a great range of genuine one-off shoes, boots and accessories designed by the owner. Accessories include bags, jewellery, belts, scarves, hats and shawls.

✉ 16 William Street ☎ 0131 220 4495; www.helenbateman.com
🚍 3, 4, 12, 25

DEPARTMENT STORES
Harvey Nichols
The 2002 opening of Harvey Nichols' third store put Edinburgh shopping right up in the style-wars lead. The shop is a world-fashion lifestyle icon and its arrival has spun off to effect huge improvements in the capital's other leading stores. Situated over five floors, this luxury designer destination is a definite must for fashion addicts, food lovers and those who take their beauty brands seriously.

✉ 30–34 St Andrew Square ☎ 0131 524 8388; www.harveynichols.com
🚍 8, 10,11, 12, 16

Jenners
Once the world's oldest independent department store, founded in 1838, Jenners has six floors of high-quality goods. This classy institution has instore restaurants, an air of old-fashioned courtesy and decor to match.

✉ 48 Princes Street ☎ 0844 800 3725; www.houseoffraser.co.uk 🚍 3, 11, 23, 24, 27, 44

FOOD AND DRINK
Valvona and Crolla
This delicatessen and wine merchant, an independent family business, is an Edinburgh institution that provides the very best of all things Italian.

✉ 19 Elm Row ☎ 0131 556 6066; www.valvonacrolla.co.uk 🚍 7, 10, 11, 12, 14

JEWELLERY
Joseph Bonnar
An attractive shop renowned for the variety and prices on offer. It has Scotland's largest range of antique jewellery.

✉ 72 Thistle Street ☎ 0131 226 2811; www.josephbonnar.com
🚍 23, 27, 29, 42

SPECIALIST
Studio One
This West End shop is known for unusual gifts, furnishings and household items in a basement setting.

✉ 10–16 Stafford Street ☎ 0131 226 5812 🚌 12, 25, 44

The Thrie Estaits
Whether you're on the lookout for a memorable antique as a souvenir, or merely want to wonder at the diversity here, the enthusiastic owners will do their best to help.

✉ 49 Dundas Street ☎ 0131 556 7084; www.thethrieestaits.co.uk 🚌 23, 27

ENTERTAINMENT

CULTURAL VENUES
Assembly Rooms
This popular venue, with its central location, makes it an ideal host for mainstream Festival Fringe productions. There is a choice of four impressive rooms including a ballroom and music hall. Ceilidhs, dances, exhibitions and gigs are held throughout the year (► 114).

✉ 54 George Street ☎ 0131 220 4348; box office: 0131 228 1155; www.assemblyroomsedinburgh.co.uk 🚌 19, 23, 37, 41

Edinburgh Playhouse
The multipurpose auditorium can stage West End musicals, concerts of all sizes and leading rock groups. It also plays host to Edinburgh International Festival performances including ballet and classical music. It is located right next door to the Vue multiscreen cinema.

✉ 18–22 Greenside Place ☎ 0844 847 1660; www.edinburgh-playhouse.co.uk 🚌 10, 11, 12, 26, 49

Jamie's Scottish Evening
The long-running dinner show, hosted by the Thistle Hotel, is a fusion of a full theatrical show and a casual Scottish ceilidh. Enjoy traditional Scottish cuisine, served with complimentary wine and be entertained by some of the best musicians and dancers. You

will learn all about Scottish history and may even witness the Ceremony of the Haggis.

✉ Thistle Hotel, 107 Leith Street ☎ 0131 556 0111; www.thistle.com
🕐 Apr–Nov nightly from 7pm 🚌 1, 5, 7, 14, 19, 22, 25, 34

Ross Open Air Theatre

An open-air seasonal venue situated in Princes Street Gardens, staging a variety of performances in the summer, including children's shows, music and dance. An Edinburgh Festival venue.

✉ Princes Street Gardens ☎ 0131 228 8616 🚌 3, 10, 17, 23, 27, 44

The Stand Comedy Club

Stand-up comedy with international routines presented with a Scottish slant. A resident team backs up acts selected from the best of today's Scottish comedians. Edinburgh Festival venue.

✉ 5 York Place ☎ 0131 558 7272 (box office); www.thestand.co.uk
🚌 10, 11, 12, 15, 26, 44

TOURS
City Bus Tours

You can get a real taste of Edinburgh by using one of the guided tour services that leave from Waverley Station and go around all the main sights. All operate a "jump on and off" policy, so the ticket price allows you to visit something, then join a later bus. Some have a lively commentary from a knowledgeable local guide, others have headphones (usually in several languages).

Edinburgh Bus Tours

Operates a range of tour buses, including open-top services.

✉ Waverley Bridge ☎ 0131 220 0770; www.edinburghtour.com

WINE BAR
Whigham's Wine Bar

This series of candlelit basement vaults off Charlotte Square supplies the perfect environment for chilling out to relaxing music, with good food and wines.

✉ 13 Hope Street ☎ 0131 225 8674 🚌 19, 37, 41

Around Edinburgh

It's certainly worth looking beyond the city centre when making a visit to Edinburgh. Within a short bus ride or a reasonable walk there are some lovely leafy suburbs, as well as parks and small villages.

Walking a little to the north, but still in New Town, are the charming streets of Stockbridge, with good restaurants and shops. To the west is Dean with its art galleries and the spectacular Water of Leith. To the south of the city is the gentle suburb of Morningside and just to the southeast is the village of Duddingston. A bus ride to the west brings you to Murrayfield and also to the excellent Edinburgh Zoo. Around 3km (2 miles) to the north and easily accessible by bus is the old docks area of Leith, now gentrified with trendy restaurants, a huge shopping mall and the Royal Yacht *Britannia*. These are just a few of the choices, so take your pick and explore.

ANN STREET

The early 19th-century construction of the Raeburn Estate, built between New Town (➤ 44–45) and the residential district of Stockbridge at the bottom of the slopes of New Town, was instrumental in bringing new wealth down the hill as the rich moved in, occupying roads such as Ann Street. Now one of Edinburgh's most exclusive addresses, its attraction lies in its scale, almost miniature compared to the grandeur of the New Town. Each house in this classically inspired terrace of perfectly proportioned houses is fronted by a garden, producing a beguiling mix of small-scale architectural splendour and cottagey charm.

➕ *Greater City 4c* ✉ Ann Street 🚌 29, 37, 41, 42

BLACKFORD HILL

Blackford Hill, south of the middle of the city, is seen at its best on uncrowded weekdays, and is a good place to head for an afternoon's fresh air, exercise and some splendid city views. Its 164m (538ft) summit is an easy climb from the surrounding parkland, up grassy slopes covered with bright yellow gorse. From here, the green southern suburbs stretch north, with Arthur's Seat over to the right and Edinburgh Castle ahead. You'll also find the Royal Observatory Edinburgh (➤ 149) on Blackford Hill. Head downhill to the wooded path that winds beside the Braid Burn to a castellated 18th-century villa known as the Hermitage of Braid. It is now a countryside information office, which will fill you in on the surprisingly wide range of wildlife to be found in the area.

➕ *Greater City 4e* ✉ Blackford 🚌 24, 38, 41

BRAID HILLS

If you're fit, you could combine a walk on Blackford Hill with a few more miles over the Braid Hills (205m/672ft) which lie just to the south and are linked to Blackford by good paths. Much of the area is covered by golf courses (➤ 161); these were laid out by the City of Edinburgh in 1889 as public courses when play on central

Bruntsfield Links was becoming restricted. Few tourists penetrate these outer hills, outliers of the Pentlands, and the only people you're likely to meet are local golfers and dog-walkers. There are more sweeping panoramas from Braid; on a clear day look north and to your left for a fine view of the Forth Bridges.

➕ *Greater City 4e* ✉ Braid Hills 🚌 24, 38, 41

THE COLONIES

Downstream from Stockbridge, the Water of Leith walkway
(➤ 153) will lead to you to one of Edinburgh's more picturesque

corners, a quiet cluster of streets of artisans' houses tucked away at the foot of the New Town heights Here you will find the 11 parallel rows of terraced houses known as The Colonies, running at right angles to the Water of Leith. This development was constructed by the Edinburgh Co-operative Building Company in 1861 for local workmen and their families. Each house is divided into upper and lower dwellings, with outside stairs to the top flats and tiny gardens. Many of the houses are decorated with plaques depicting the tools used by the tradesmen involved in their construction – masons, plumbers, joiners, plasterers and decorators.

➕ *Greater City 4c* ✉ Stockbridge 🚌 29

CRAIGMILLAR CASTLE

You'll have to brave some of Edinburgh's poorer housing schemes
to reach Craigmillar Castle, one of Scotland's most impressive
medieval remains, standing in fields on the southeast side of the
city. The L-plan tower dates from the mid- to late 15th century and
stands in a courtyard surrounded by curtain walls complete with
massive corner towers. The castle was a favourite with Mary,
Queen of Scots, and one of the two barrel-vaulted chambers is
known as Queen Mary's Room. She fled to Craigmillar, "wishing
herself dead", after the murder of her secretary and favourite,
David Rizzio, at Holyrood in 1566. Craigmillar later passed to the
Gilmour family, who placed it in state care in 1946. Most children
enjoy its empty spaces more than the packed precincts of
Edinburgh's other, more famous castle.

www.historic-scotland.gov.uk

✚ *Greater City 6e* ✉ Craigmillar Castle Road ☎ 0131 661 4445
🕔 Apr–Sep daily 9:30–5:30; Oct daily 9:30–4:30; Nov–Mar Mon–Wed,
Sat–Sun 9:30–4:30 🖐 Moderate 🚌 2, 14

CRAMOND

For a change from city sights, it's well worth making the short
journey out to Cramond, a picturesque suburb on the shores of the
Firth of Forth to the northwest of the city. Cramond was founded

by the Romans, who established a harbour at the mouth of the River Almond in the 2nd century as a base for the soldiers constructing the Antonine Wall. Sections of the Roman fort, including a well-preserved bath-house, have been excavated, and an impressive Roman sculpture of a lion was found near the water's edge in 1997. Cramond has attractive 16th-century houses, some later, elegant villas, a famous inn and a cruciform church, from 1656. During the 18th century, Cramond's river position led to the establishment of four iron mills along the Almond; Scotland's first commercially produced steel came from here.

Today, you can follow the River Almond Walkway upriver or walk beside the shore of the Firth of Forth. Offshore lies Cramond Island, a grassy tidal island accessible at low tide if you don't mind scrambling over the slippery rocks and blocks of the causeway. Beware of the fast tides which sometimes catch people out. Across the river lies **Dalmeny House,** which has miles of parkland walks (accessible July and August) and a delightful but long shore walk (via Cramond Brig) to South Queensferry (accessible all year). On your way back into the city, **Lauriston Castle** is worth a visit; this 16th-century tower house, built for Sir Archibold Napier, was extended in the 1820s and has fine Edwardian interiors reflecting the wealth of middle-class collectors of the period.

✚ Greater City 2c

Dalmeny House

✉ Cramond ☎ 0131 331 1888; www.dalmeny.co.uk
🅖 Park: unlimted access all year 🍴 Cramond Inn (£–££; ▶ 58) 🚍 40, 41

Lauriston Castle

✉ Cramond Road South, Davidson's Mains ☎ 0131 336 2060; www.cac.org.uk 🅖 Apr–Oct Sat–Thu, tours 11:20–4:20; Nov–Mar Sat–Sun, tours at 2 ✋ Expensive (free access to grounds) 🚍 21, 24, 41 ❓ Many indoor and outdoor events between spring and Christmas. Full details from Lauriston Castle

DEAN VILLAGE

Thomas Telford's Dean Bridge spans the steep gorge of the Water of Leith, marking the northern limit of Edinburgh's New Town. Lying 32m (105ft) below the bridge is Dean Village, a quiet and historic enclave with attractive old houses and easy access to the river. In medieval times the Dean was Edinburgh's milling area, with 11 mills operating. Several 19th-century mill buildings survive, now converted into apartments – look for Well Court, originally built as housing for workers in 1884. Baxter's Tolbooth is a 17th-century granary. Across the river Dean Cemetery overlooks the village. This 19th-century graveyard contains some of Edinburgh's finest funerary monuments, the best of them designed by William Playfair, the New Town architect, who is also buried here.

➕ *Greater City 4c* ✉ Dean Village 🚌 19, 37, 41

DUDDINGSTON

Crouched in the shadow of Arthur's Seat, the ancient settlement of Duddingston is one of Edinburgh's most attractive corners. Its pretty streets run down to Duddingston Loch, now part of a bird sanctuary and always thronged with geese and other wildfowl. This is the loch purportedly featured in the National Gallery's famous picture of the Reverend Walker skating (► 43). Duddingston Kirk is a 12th-century foundation, still retaining its Norman doorway and beautifully set in a verdant churchyard. Take time to wander around before heading for a drink in the Sheep Heid Inn, dating from at least 1580 when it was patronized by James VI; it has the oldest skittle alley in Scotland.

➕ *Greater City 6d* ✉ Duddingston 🍴 Sheep Heid Inn (£–££) 🚌 44

EDINBURGH ZOO

Spreading up the slopes of Corstorphine Hill, Edinburgh Zoo is the headquarters of the Royal Scottish Zoological Society, with a strong accent on conservation, captive breeding of endangered species and education. With more than 1,000 animals from across the world, plenty of hands-on opportunities and activities; it is child-friendly. Kids will enjoy the chance to see rhinoceros, bears, giraffes, zebras, hippos and many more. The lion enclosure is popular, and there's the Magic Forest, devoted to small rainforest monkeys. The highlight for most visitors is the daily penguin parade at 2:15pm; the zoo successfully breeds four species of these charming birds, which you can see swimming underwater through the glass windows of their pool. Be prepared to climb – the hill is steep though there are free truck rides to the highest point.

www.edinburghzoo.org.uk

🚩 *Greater City 2d* ✉ Murrayfield ☎ 0131 334 9171 🕐 Apr–Sep, daily 9–6; Oct, Mar 9–5; Nov–Feb 9–4:30 ✋ Expensive 🍴 Cafes and kiosks (£–££) 🚌 12, 26 ❓ Many special events aimed specifically at children

LEITH

There's been less-than-friendly rivalry between Leith and Edinburgh over the centuries, dating from the days when the latter controlled all Leith's foreign trade – indeed, Leith was only amalgamated with the capital in 1920. Its history as a dock area dates from before the 14th century, though its existing docks and warehouses mainly went up in the 1800s. Leith's dock area now boasts Ocean Terminal, one of Europe's largest shopping and leisure development, with three floors of shops, bars and restaurants, and a multiscreen cinema. This is one more sign of Leith's regeneration over recent years. A trip by bus down Leith

Walk, which links it to the city, is a good option for a change of pace, although it is rather run-down these days.

Head first for the Shore, a restored area by the Water of Leith, with excellent bars and restaurants. Leith now has three Michelin-star restaurants. Nearby warehouses have been converted to smart accommodation; you can see these on Commercial Street, which gives access to the quay where the Royal Yacht *Britannia* (➤ 150) is moored. The impressive postmodern building housing the Scottish Office also draws the eye. East of the Shore several older buildings have survived near the Kirkgate, the old town area, spoiled by a disastrous shopping arcade and high-rise apartments. Leith Links lies farther east again, a pleasant green space. The Links claims to be one of the earliest homes of golf; the ground was in use for golf in 1593 and it was here that the first set of rules was formulated.

✚ *Greater City 5b* ✉ Leith 🍴 Skippers (££; ➤ 158) 🚌 1, 11, 22, 34, 35, 36

MORNINGSIDE

Tucked away in the quiet, leafy streets of Morningside on the southwest side of Edinburgh are solid Victorian villas still housing the prosperous citizens of Edinburgh's middle classes. Morningside, its respectability the butt of countless jokes, is one of several suburbs developed in the 19th century for the growing bourgeoisie, who wanted to live neither in the cold grandeur of the New Town nor the increasing squalor of the Old. The area is approached via "Holy Corner", the affectionate local name for a crossroads surrounded by no less than four churches. Morningside, with its range of good shops, services and local amenities, has all a suburb could wish for; a stroll round here provides that insight into local life which is often so hard to find in major cities.

✠ *Greater City 4e* ✉ Morningside 🚌 5, 11, 16, 17, 23

MURRAYFIELD

The western suburb of Murrayfield, all terraces and villas, was developed around 18th-century Murrayfield House in the 1860s. It's a well-to-do area with good local amenities and easy access both to the city and Corstorphine Hill. Twice a year Murrayfield comes into its own as crowds pour into Murrayfield Stadium, home of Scotland's international rugby union team, where home games are played during the Six Nations championship. The stadium, extended and modernized over the years, was built in 1925 by the then Scottish Football Union. The first game was played in March that year – Scotland beat England 14–11.

✠ *Greater City 3d* ✉ Murrayfield ☎ Murrayfield Stadium 0131 346 5000; www.murrayfieldexperience.com 🚌 12, 26, 31

ROYAL BOTANIC GARDEN
Best places to see, ➤ 50–51.

ROYAL OBSERVATORY EDINBURGH
The Royal Observatory Edinburgh moved from Calton Hill (➤ 114) in 1895 when light pollution was starting to interfere with observations from the central site. This is still very much a working observatory, charged with the task of collating material for astronomers worldwide from the UK's telescopes here and overseas, and housing sophisticated equipment. The excellent visitor facility opens for pre-booked group visits and special events. The roof terrace has far-reaching views north to the heart of the city; if you're in Edinburgh during the winter, there are weekly Friday-evening viewing sessions at the observatory and a varied programme of winter talks starts each October.

www.roe.ac.uk

✤ *Greater City 4e* ✉ Blackford Hill ☎ 0131 668 8404 ⓘ Observing evenings: 7–8:45pm, booking essential 🖐 Moderate 🚌 24, 38, 41

THE ROYAL YACHT *BRITANNIA*

In 1953 the ocean-going Royal Yacht *Britannia* was launched on Clydebank in Scotland. She remained in service for more than 40 years, travelling more than a million miles to every corner of the world on voyages that included 968 official and state visits, family holidays and royal honeymoons. For the Queen and her family *Britannia* was "home", a place to work, entertain and relax. Now fully restored and moored at Leith, *Britannia* still contains the fittings, furnishings, paintings and photographs from her working days. Tours start in the visitor centre, where exhibits and film tell the yacht's story. From here visitors follow a route round the yacht with an audio handset explaining the different areas on show. These include the bridge, the Queen's bedroom and sitting room, the splendid dining room, the decks and the engine room.
www.royalyachtbritannia.co.uk

✚ *Greater City 5b* ✉ Ocean Terminal, Leith ☎ 0131 555 5566 🕓 Jan–Mar, Nov, Dec daily 10–5; Apr–Jun, Sep, Oct 10–5:30; Jul 9:30–5:30; Aug 9:30–6 ✋ Expensive 🍴 Cafe in visitor centre (£–££) 🚌 1, 11, 22, 34, 35, 36 direct from Waverley Bridge ❓ Booking strongly advised

ST MARY'S EPISCOPAL CATHEDRAL

In 1870, the Misses Barbara and Mary Coates, devoted Episcopalians, left a legacy in the shape of land and money for the building of a cathedral in the West End of Edinburgh. St Mary's, with the sisters' 17th-century mansion still in its shadow, is the result, a soaring Victorian Gothic creation that dominates this part of the city. Designed by Sir George Gilbert Scott and built between 1874 and 1879, it is a cruciform church whose central tower rises to 84m (276ft) – the full effect is best seen from Melville Street. The twin western towers were added in 1917, and are affectionately known as Barbara and Mary, in memory of the cathedral's donors. The interior combines architectural sobriety with a pious cosiness; look out for the glowing murals by Phoebe Anna Traquair, a leading figure in the Arts and Crafts movement.

✝ *Greater City 4d* ✉ Palmerston Place ☎ 0131 225 6293; www.cathedral.net ⏱ Daily 7:15–6 (9pm in summer) ✋ Free 🚌 3, 13, 25, 31, 33 ❓ Regular organ recitals and concerts; choral evensong during term time. Phone cathedral for information

SCOTTISH NATIONAL GALLERY OF MODERN ART AND THE DEAN GALLERY

An afternoon in Edinburgh's superbly designed modern art galleries makes a fascinating contrast to medieval and Georgian Edinburgh. In 1999 Edinburgh's permanent exhibition space for modern art doubled with the opening of the Dean Gallery. The two galleries lie on either side of Belford Road, the Gallery of Modern Art housed in a 19th-century neoclassical former school, the Dean in an earlier ex-hospital. The Gallery of Modern Art has a fine collection of international and Scottish 20th-century art, with examples of Fauvism, expressionism, and Surrealism including works by Francis Bacon and Jackson Pollock. The Dean contains Edinburgh's Dada and Surrealist collection, as well as many works by Eduardo Paolozzi, the Scottish sculptor whose work you may also have seen in the National Museum of Scotland (➤ 40–41).

www.nationalgalleries.org

✝ *Greater City 3d* ✉ Belford Road ☎ 0131 624 6200 ⏱ Daily 10–5 ✋ Free 🍴 Cafe in Gallery of Modern Art (£–££), Café Newton in Dean Gallery (£) 🚌 13, free bus links all five national galleries ❓ Charges for special exhibitions

STOCKBRIDGE

Situated at the bottom of the slopes of New Town, the lively residential district of Stockbridge was once a milling and tanning village lying alongside the Water of Leith (➤ 153) and was the access point for livestock entering the city. In 1786 the present stone bridge was built and over the next 100 years Stockbridge gradually merged with Edinburgh as the tenement buildings, trim terraces and genteel villas went up. By the 1970s the area was crumbling, ripe for students, artists and the first alternative lifestylers, who moved in attracted by the low rents. In their wake came shops and restaurants, gentrification followed and Stockbridge once more became a desirable place to live. It's an alluring mélange of smart and cosy, where traditional foodshops rub shoulders with trendy bars and designer outlets. Make for St Stephen's Street to get a lingering taste of 1970s Stockbridge, before heading along the water's edge-footpath to explore the Water of Leith.

✚ *Greater City 4c* ✉ Stockbridge
🚌 23, 27, 29, 36

SWANSTON

Driving is the simplest way to get to Swanston, perhaps the prettiest of all Edinburgh's "villages" and barely part of the city at all. Separated from the urban sprawl by the southern bypass and lying on the slopes of the Pentlands, the middle of this conservation village has changed very little since the 19th century. A group of thatched cottages clusters round the village green together with the original 18th-century farmhouse and old school. Swanston is best known for its links with author Robert Louis Stevenson; he came to spend the summers here with his family and nurse from 1867 to 1880.

✚ *Greater City 4f* ✉ Swanston 🚌 5, 17, 27 followed by walk

THE WATER OF LEITH

The Water of Leith runs for more than 32km (20 miles) through a string of suburbs and Edinburgh itself to reach the Firth of Forth at Leith. Most of its course is a gentle meander, with more dramatic scenery at Dean (➤ 144), where the water has carved its way through a deep gorge. For hundreds of years the banks were lined with mills, with up to 80 on the bottom stretch in the early 1800s. A walkway (21km/13 miles) follows the path of the river from Balerno to Leith, a good way to explore the area.

The nicest stretch by far is focused around the village of Stockbridge (➤ 152); this agreeable walk (➤ 154–155) gives access upriver to the Scottish National Gallery of Modern Art (➤ 151) and downstream to the Royal Botanic Garden (➤ 50–51). Alternatively, follow the last stages of the Water through Leith, where you'll see some 17th- and 18th-century warehouses and merchants' houses near the Water's end at the docks.

✚ *Greater City 3d* ✉ Runs from Balerno to Leith with access at different points 🚌 Balerno 44; Leith 10, 11, 22, 36

ℹ 24 Lanark Road (near Balerrno) ☎ 0131 455 7367 🕐 Daily 10–4 🚌 44

a walk through the Water of Leith

*From Queensferry Street turn left
steeply down Bell's Brae to join the
Water of Leith Walkway in Dean Village.*

This is a good opportunity to explore the
village (➤ 144).

*Walk downstream, under the soaring
Dean Bridge to reach St Bernard's Well.*

This elegant columned temple, with its
statue of the Roman goddess Hygeia,
marks the sulphurous mineral springs of
St Bernard's Well, discovered by three
schoolboys in the 1760s. It quickly became
popular as a place of healing. The wellhouse was designed
by Alexander Nasmyth in 1789.

*Turn left and cross the river, then right down Dean
Terrace to the centre of Stockbridge (➤ 152). Cross
Deanhaugh Street and rejoin the riverside path. Continue
to Bridge Place, then cross the road and turn right up
Arboretum Avenue. As the river curves, turn right along
Rocheid Path.*

You are now opposite the rows of
streets known as The Colonies
(➤ 141).

*Follow the path down Inverleith
Terrace Lane and turn left into
Inverleith Row. After 183m (200yds)
turn left to enter the Royal Botanic
Garden (➤ 50–51) and walk*

through by whichever route you like to Arboretum Place on the west side of the gardens. Cross the road and walk straight through Inverleith Park to Fettes Avenue.

The soaring and ornate building in front of you is Fettes College, the school where the former prime minister, Tony Blair, was educated.

Turn left down Fettes Avenue and continue, then turn left at the junction with Comely Bank Road, which becomes Raeburn Place.

Distance 4.8km (3 miles)
Time 1.5 hours walking; 2–2.5 with visit to Royal Botanic Garden
Start Point Queensferry Street ✚ 1D 🚌 13, 19, 29, 37, 41
End Point Raeburn Place ✚ 1A 🚌 19, 24, 29, 42
Lunch The Terrace Café (£) ✉ Royal Botanical Garden, Inverleith Row ☎ 0131 552 0616

HOTELS

Abbotsford Guest House (£)

Just north of New Town, and within reasonable walking distance of the city centre, this charming and friendly guest house offers individually decorated, pleasantly furnished and thoughtfully equipped bedrooms. There is an elegant ground-floor dining room where hearty breakfasts are served at individual tables.

✉ 36 Pilrig Street ☎ 0131 554 2706; www.abbotsfordguesthouse.co.uk 🚌 11

Best Western Braid Hills (£££)

This long-established hotel enjoys panoramic views across Edinburgh. Bedrooms are smart, stylish and well equipped, and there's a choice of the restaurant or brasserie and bar. Two rooms have four-poster beds.

✉ 134 Braid Road ☎ 0131 447 8888; www.braidhillshotel.co.uk 🚌 11, 15

Best Western Bruntsfield Hotel (££–£££)

This large Victorian town house, 1km (0.5 miles) south of Princes Street, has good views over Bruntsfield Links and offers good service and a conservatory-style restaurant.

✉ 69 Bruntsfield Place ☎ 0131 229 1393; www.thebruntsfield.co.uk 🚌 16, 17, 23

Dunstane House (£–££)

This fine Victorian mansion, close to Haymarket Station, offers friendly service. Rooms are elegant and well-equipped and there is a residents' bar offering a selection of Scottish whiskies.

✉ 4 West Coates, Haymarket ☎ 0131 337 6169; www.dunstane-hotel-edinburgh.co.uk 🚌 12, 26, 31

Malmaison (£££)

An old seaman's mission at Leith houses this classic contemporary hotel with individually designed rooms. Deservedly popular for its great waterfront views, and with a good art nouveau-style French brasserie.

✉ 1 Tower Place ☎ 0131 468 5000; www.malmaison.com 🚌 16, 22, 35, 36

RESTAURANTS

The Canny Man's (££)

An excellent family-run pub with a great reputation for superb seafood, beef and wine. Reservations are advised.

✉ 237 Morningside Road ☎ 0131 447 1484 ⏰ Mon–Fri 12–3, 6:30–9, Sat 12–3, Sun 12:30–3 🚌 5, 11, 17, 23

Chop Chop (££)

This fantastic neighbourhood Chinese was massively popular even before appearing on Gordon Ramsay's F Word – a popular TV programme looking for Britain's best local restaurants – and having its world-class dim sum stocked by Sainsbury's, a leading supermarket. Mercifully fame has not ruined the busy ambience and laid-back service of this canteen-style eatery, and the North Chinese cooking remains first rate.

✉ 248 Morrison Street ☎ 0131 221 1155 ⏰ Tue–Fri 12–2, 5:30–10:30, Sat–Sun 5–11; closed Mon 🚌 2

Cramond Inn (£–££)

See page 58.

Daniel's Bistro (££)

See page 58.

Kitchin (£££)

Tom Kitchin's superb restaurant well deserves its Michelin star. This TV chef promotes fresh local produce and seasonality and this translates strongly in his inspirational cooking.

✉ 78 Commercial Quay, Leith ☎ 0131 555 1755; www.thekitchin.com ⏰ Tue–Thu 12:30–1:45, 7–10, Fri–Sat 12:30–1:45, 6:45–10 🚌 16, 22, 35

Loon Fung (££)

Popular Canonmills restaurant serving a wide range of Cantonese specialities, incorporating fish, meat and vegetarian dishes, in a friendly atmosphere.

✉ 2 Warriston Place ☎ 0131 556 1781 ⏰ Mon–Thu 12–11:30, Fri 12–12, Sat 2–12, Sun 2–11:30 🚌 8, 23, 36

Montpeliers (££)

This stylish Bruntsfield bistro is open all day for its tempting breakfasts, international lunch and dinner dishes and speciality cocktails.

✉ 159–161 Bruntsfield Place ☎ 0131 229 3115; www.montpeliers.co.uk
🕐 Daily 9am–1am 🚌 11, 17, 23

Plumed Horse (£££)

Tony Borthwick's Michelin-star dining room is the setting for seriously grand cooking. Local produce features heavily on a menu that offers dishes such as Gressingham duck and wild halibut. The desserts, such as hot strawberry soufflé are equally impressive.

✉ 50–54 Henderson Street, Leith ☎ 0131 554 5556;
www.plumedhorse.co.uk 🕐 Tue–Sat 12–1:30, 7–9 🚌 16, 22, 35

Restaurant Martin Wishart (£££)

Edinburgh's hot choice for the very best of modern European cuisine. Expect daily changing menus, laid-back formality, terrific service and some of the best food in town.

✉ 54 The Shore ☎ 0131 553 3557; www.martin-wishart.co.uk 🕐 Tue–Sat
12–2, 7–10 🚌 16, 22, 35, 36

Rhubarb (£££)

Dine in style at a 17th-century mansion in the shadow of Arthur's Seat. Franco-Scottish cooking and an award-winning wine cellar.

✉ Prestonfield, Priestfield Road ☎ 0131 225 1333; www.prestonfield.com
🕐 Daily 12–3, 6–11 🚌 Take a taxi

The Shore Bar and Restaurant (££)

See page 59.

Skippers (££)

A leading seafood bistro for 30 years in a great waterside location serving delicious, locally sourced fish specialities. Book in advance.

✉ 1a Dock Place, Leith ☎ 0131 554 1018; www.skippers.co.uk 🕐 Daily
12:30–2, 7–10 🚌 16, 22, 35, 36

SHOPPING

ANTIQUES
The Courtyard Antiques
Spread across two floors with all sorts of bric-a-brac, the highlights of this shop are the vintage toys, though the range they manage to cram in is perhaps more impressive.

✉ 108a Causewayside ☎ 0131 447 9008 🚌 3, 7, 31

CLOTHING AND WOOLLENS
Highlander
Cheaper and less touristy than the kilt purveyors of the Royal Mile. Here you can hire full Highland dress or even get fitted out for a bespoke outfit to take home with you. It's good value for money and worth the bus journey if you are serious about your kilt.

✉ 6 Hutchison Terrace, Chesser Avenue ☎ 0131 455 7505; www.highlanderkilthire.com 🚌 35

Kinloch Anderson
Every aspect of traditional Highland dress is available here.

✉ Commercial Street/Dock Street, Leith ☎ 0131 555 1390; www.kinlochanderson.com 🚌 16, 22, 25, 36

SPECIALITY FOOD
IJ Mellis
Perhaps the most charming outlet of Scotland's most renowned cheesemonger. It stocks a superb range of Scottish cheese (the Dunsyre and Lanark blues are world class) and a selection from around the UK and Ireland. Other deli goodies are on sale, so it's a great spot to put together a picnic to have in the nearby Meadows.

✉ 330 Morningside Road ☎ 0131 447 8889; www.mellischeese.co.uk 🚌 11, 23

Peckhams
The place for MacSween's award-winning haggis, considered to be the best, along with a myriad other specialities.

✉ 155–159 Bruntsfield Place ☎ 0131 229 7054; www.peckhams.co.uk 🚌 11, 15, 16, 23

ENTERTAINMENT

CINEMAS
Dominion Cinema

This old-fashioned cinema shows the latest releases in comfort and style. Situated in Morningside on the south side of the city.
✉ 18 Newbattle Terrace ☎ 0131 447 4771; recorded information: 0131 447 2660; www.dominioncinemas.net 🚌 5, 11, 15, 16, 23

CULTURAL VENUES
Church Hill Theatre

This municipal theatre is a popular venue for professional companies during the Festival. It is also home to many amateur theatre companies who perform here the rest of the year.
✉ 33 Morningside Road ☎ 0131 447 7597 🚌 5, 11, 15, 16

PUBS
King's Wark

A great locals' pub overlooking the Water of Leith. Enjoy Scottish ales or try some excellent cooking in the adjacent dining section. Some of Edinburgh's best pub meals served in the bar too.
✉ 36 The Shore, Leith ☎ 0131 554 9260 🚌 16, 22, 35

The Roseleaf

Arty but unpretentious pub that cuts to the heart of the Bohemian spirit of trendy Leith. Laze away the day with local artists, admire their work on the walls and enjoy the banter with the quirky staff.
✉ 23–25 Sandport Place, Leith ☎ 0131 476 5266; www.roseleaf.co.uk
🚌 16, 22, 35

SPORT

ATHLETICS
Meadowbank Sports Centre and Stadium

This is the city's main venue for athletics meetings. As well as a velodome, it also offers facilities for squash, basketball and badminton in a series of indoor halls, and has a climbing frame.
✉ 139 London Road ☎ 0131 661 5351; www.edinburghleisure.co.uk
🚌 5, 26, 44

CLIMBING
Edinburgh International Climbing Arena
The climbing arena at Ratho offers indoor climbing and a variety of coaching sessions for climbers of all levels. For younger children there is Scrambles – an excellent soft play area.

✉ Ratho Quarry, South Platt Hill, Ratho, Newbridge ☎ 0131 333 6333; www.eica-ratho.com

GOLF
Braid Hills Golf Course
Golfers enjoy the bonus of having superb views of Edinburgh and the Firth of Forth from this challenging and hilly course to the south of the city.

✉ Braid Hills Approach ☎ 0131 447 6666; www.edinburghleisure.co.uk
🚌 11, 15

Craigmillar Park Golf Course
Close to the Royal Observatory (➤ 149), this private 18-hole parkland course welcomes visitors on week days and weekends, by arrangement, to play over its sloping holes.

✉ 1 Observatory Road ☎ 0131 667 0047; www.craigmillarpark.co.uk
🚌 24, 38, 41

Silverknowes Golf Course
This municipally owned course is pleasantly situated close to the Firth of Forth, and the gently undulating terrain presents some challenging holes for local golfers and visitors.

✉ Silverknowes Parkway ☎ 0131 336 3843; www.edinburghleisure.co.uk
🚌 16, 27, 42

HORSE-RACING
Musselburgh Racecourse
This racecourse is 10km (6 miles) east of Edinburgh beside the Firth of Forth. More than 20 events are held during the year, both flat racing and jump meetings.

✉ Linkfield Road ☎ 0131 665 2859; www.musselburgh-racecourse.co.uk
🚌 15, 15A

Excursions

Using Edinburgh as a base, it's possible to get a real taste of the diversity of Scotland – its spectacular scenery, dramatic coastline, forbidding castles and grand mansions, attractive villages and ancient towns. Within a few hours' drive, north or south, you can experience a wealth of different sights, which do much to put the city into perspective as the country's capital.

Central Scotland is home to the majority of Scots, with good roads and transport links, much of Scotland's industry and an increasing sense of purpose and hope for the future. Equally, some of the country's best agricultural land lies near at hand, while the hills, lochs and rivers offer the chance to appreciate a sense of space. Glasgow's dynamism stands in contrast to the tranquillity of the Fife and Borders villages, while its rich cultural life and history are further assets which will add to your Edinburgh experience.

GLASGOW

Glasgow, Scotland's largest city, lies a mere 80km (50 miles) from Edinburgh, a city so different in heritage, atmosphere and style that it might as well be 10 times the distance. Industrial Glasgow, decaying 40 years ago, is now one of Britain's most go-ahead cities, with superb 19th-century architecture and a tangible atmosphere of dynamism. Go there to enjoy the contrast with Edinburgh, the buzz of its designer stores, restaurants and museums, and the wonderful friendliness of its people.

www.seeglasgow.com

➕ *Greater City inset map 6b* ✉ 73km (45 miles) from Edinburgh
ℹ️ 11 George Square ☎ 0141 204 4400;
Airport Tourist Information Centre, Glasgow
International Airport, Paisley ☎ 0141 848 4440

Burrell Collection

Glasgow inherited Sir William Burrell's outstanding art collections in 1944, but it was not until 1983 that a suitable home was built for them, a clean-lined stone-and-glass structure in Pollock Country Park on the south side of the city. Here you'll find paintings, furniture, sculpture and ceramics, architectural fragments and superb Egyptian, Greek, Roman and Asiatic pieces of all sorts. Art-lovers journey to Glasgow specifically to see the collection, so you need to allow plenty of time. The highlight is the huge Warwick Vase, a 2nd-century Roman marble urn on display in the courtyard.

www.glasgowmuseums.com

✉ 2060 Pollokshaws Road, Pollock Country Park ☎ 0141 287 2550
🕐 Mon–Thu, Sat 10–5, Fri, Sun 11–5 ✋ Free 🍴 Restaurant and cafe (£–££)
🚆 Pollokshaws West (10 mins walk) 🚌 First Bus 45, 47, 48, 57

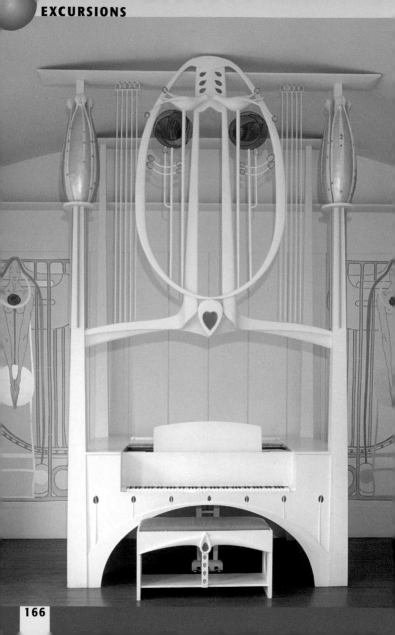

Charles Rennie Mackintosh Trail

Fans of Glasgow's most famous architect, born here in 1868, can track down some of the best examples of his work, stylistically an entirely original blend of Arts and Crafts, art nouveau and Scottish. Head for the Glasgow School of Art, still a working school and one of his best-known designs, before taking in the famous Willow Tea Rooms in Sauchiehall Street and Bellahouston Park's House for an Art Lover. Kelvingrove Museum and The Hunterian Museum each contain Mackintosh interiors, furniture and decorative objects.

🔢 Mackintosh tours are organized by the Charles Rennie Mackintosh Society, Queens Cross Church, 870 Garscube Road ☎ 0141 946 6600; www.crmsociety.com

George Square

Glasgow's grandiose George Square epitomizes the city's 19th-century industrial prosperity. Its wide expanse is dominated by the massive block of the magnificent City Chambers, which has an Italian Renaissance-style facade that gives a taste of the wonders within. Sir Walter Scott looms over it all from a 24m (79ft) column, and 10 other statues include those of Queen Victoria, Robert Burns and James Watt. Southeast from the square spreads the "Merchant City", once the focus of trading, now a booming area of chic bars, classy restaurants, and designer stores.

📷 George Square 🚇 Buchanan Street

People's Palace

There's no better place to get a feel for the social history of Glasgow than in the 1898 People's Palace, which has exhibitions devoted to all aspects of everyday and working life in the city. The museum displays are interactive and visitor-friendly. The splendid adjoining Winter Gardens were badly damaged by a fire in 1998.

✉ Glasgow Green ☎ 0141 276 0788 🕐 Mon–Thu, Sat 10–5, Fri, Sun 11–5
🎟 Free 🚌 First Bus 16, 18, 40, 61, 62, 64, 263

HADDINGTON

Set in the fertile land between the Lammermuir Hills and the coast, the royal burgh of Haddington has no less than 130 buildings listed as being of historical or architectural interest, a fine late medieval parish church, a beguilingly odd-shaped square as well as galleries, museums and enticing shops. Don't miss the alabaster Elizabethan monuments in the Lauderdale Aisle in St Mary's Church, which also houses the tomb of Jane Carlyle, wife of the historian Thomas Carlyle. Outside town, **Lennoxlove House,** seat of the Dukes of Hamilton, is one of Scotland's grandest houses, with historical relics and fine furniture, paintings and porcelain.

✚ *Greater City inset map 8a* ✉ 32km (20 miles) from Edinburgh

Lennoxlove House

✉ Lennoxlove, Haddington ☎ 01620 823720; www.lennoxlove.com
🕐 Easter–Oct Wed, Thu, Sat 2–4:30 ✋ Moderate

LINLITHGOW

Visitors to Linlithgow should head first to the **Linlithgow Story,** which relates the history of this medieval industrial area and royal burgh. **Linlithgow Palace** is the main draw, a well-preserved lochside ruin, where Mary, Queen of Scots was born in 1542. Next door stands St Michael's Church, rebuilt in 1424 and topped by an aluminium tower in the 1960s. The town is liberally dotted with fine 17th-century buildings and also boasts a stretch of the Edinburgh-Glasgow canal. The one-hour walk around Linlithgow Loch opens up the town and offers sweeping views of the palace.

✚ *Greater City inset map 7a* ✉ 29km (18 miles) from Edinburgh

Linlithgow Palace

☎ 01506 842896; www.historic-scotland.gov.uk ⏱ Apr–Sep daily 9:30–5:30; Oct–Mar 9:30–4:30 ✋ Moderate

The Linlithgow Story

✉ 143 High Street ☎ 01506 670677; www.linlithgowstory.org.uk
⏱ Easter–Oct Mon–Sat 11–5, Sun 1–4

NORTH BERWICK

North Berwick, once a fishing and trading port, is now a prosperous commuter town and holiday resort, with solid Victorian buildings, a bustling harbour, a renowned golf course, good shops, and sandy beaches and impressive coastline nearby. If you want something more energetic than a beach stroll you could tackle Berwick Law, the 187m (614ft) volcanic rock formation behind the town. Birdwatchers should head for the **Scottish Seabird Centre,** where you can see, study and learn more about the birds of the Bass Rock and of the surrounding coastline.

✚ *Greater City inset map 8a* ✉ 41km (26 miles) from Edinburgh

Scottish Seabird Centre

✉ North Berwick Harbour ☎ 01620 890202; www.seabird.org ⏱ Feb–Mar and Oct Mon–Fri 10–5, Sat–Sun 10–5:30; Apr–Sep daily 10–6; Nov–Jan Mon–Fri 10–4, Sat–Sun 10–5:30 ✋ Expensive 🚌 First Bus 124

Museum of Flight

This excellent museum is famous for one of its most recent arrivals – Concorde. This grand dame of the skies has become a major attraction. The museum also has a remarkable array of both civil and military aircraft, with everything from Comet, the jet that made commercial aviation what it is today, through to the notorious Vulcan Bomber that was forced to make an emergency landing in Brazil during the Falklands War and was impounded for a week.

www.nms.ac.uk

✚ *Greater City inset map 8a* ✉ East Fortune Airfield, East Lothian, 6.5km (4 miles) south of North Berwick ☎ 0131 247 4238 ⏱ Apr–Oct daily 10–5; Nov–Mar Sat–Sun 10–4 ✋ Expensive

Tantallon Castle

The castle at Tantallon stands on a promontory high above the sea, the entire headland protected by massive walls and earthworks. Behind, a spectacular exposed coastal view opens up, with the Bass Rock in the background. One of Scotland's most evocative ruins, Tantallon was built in the 14th century as an enclosure castle, and is little more than walls, towers and defences "enclosing" a grassy platform on the cliffs above the pounding sea. Built of local red rock, its 15m (50ft) thick walls are flanked by towers and pierced by a central gatehouse-keep. The stronghold was besieged and blockaded several times and passed in and out of the Douglas family's ownership down the years. In 1651 it was attacked by English forces under the command of General Monk, and its medieval defences proved no match for state-of-the-art, 17th-century ordnance.

🟢 *Greater City inset map 8a* ✉ 4.2km (2.6 miles) from North Berwick
☎ 01620 892727 ⏰ Apr–Sep daily 9:30–5:30; Oct–Mar Sat–Wed 9:30–4:30
♿ Moderate

PEEBLES

Peebles is a clean and couthy (friendly) riverside town beautifully set beside the Tweed and girdled with rolling hills. Antiquities include two ancient churches, a 14th-century Mercat Cross and a five-arched bridge, first built in the 15th century. The town has been a wool-manufacturing base for many years, and has plenty of wool and knitwear shops. The town's literary connections are strong; Robert Louis Stevenson lived here as a child, and John Buchan, author of *The Thirty-Nine Steps*, spent summers here with his family. Mountain bikers should check out the world-class facilities at nearby **Glentress.** It offers rides for all abilities, bike and gear hire and a cafe on site.

✚ *Greater City inset map 7b* ✉ 38km (26.6 miles) from Edinburgh 🚩 High Street ☎ 0870 6080404 🕐 Mon–Sat 10–5, Sun 10–2

Glentress, by Peebles

✉ The Hub, Glentress Forest, Peebles ☎ 01721 721 736; www.thehubintheforest.co.uk 🍴 Cafe (£)

Neidpath Castle

It's a pleasant walk along the Tweed from the middle of Peebles to Neidpath Castle, an imposing turreted structure set on a rocky outcrop above a bend of the River Tweed. This 14th-century L-plan tower house has passed from the Frasers via the Hays, Douglases and Scotts to the Earls of Wemyss, who restored it in the 19th century. Children enjoy exploring the castle with its pit prison and small museum, and you can picnic in the grounds or by the river below.

✚ *Greater City inset map 7b* ✉ Peebles ☎ 01721 720333 🕐 Easter weekend and May–Sep Wed–Sat 10:30–5, Sun 12:30–5 ✋ Moderate

ROSSLYN CHAPEL

For a glimpse of some of Britain's finest medieval stone carving head for Rosslyn Chapel, well known to readers of *The Da Vinci Code* by Dan Brown. Founded in 1447 by William Sinclair, the 3rd Earl of Orkney, the chapel was intended to form part of a huge collegiate church dedicated to St Michael, which was never built. Only 21m (69ft) long, the entire chapel is profusely carved with intricate and sophisticated sculptures, entwined with flowers and foliage. Most famous is the so-called Prentice Pillar, said to have been carved by an apprentice while his master was away; so fine was the pupil's work that his master killed him out of jealousy on his return.

www.rosslynchapel.org.uk

➕ *Greater City inset map 7b* ✉ Roslin, Midlothian, 14km (8.5 miles) from Edinburgh ☎ 0131 440 2159 🕓 Apr–Sep Mon–Sat 9:30–6, Sun 12–4:45; Oct–Mar Mon–Sat 9:30–5, Sun 12–4:45 ✋ Expensive

SOUTH QUEENSFERRY

The picturesque suburb of South Queensferry lies on the banks of the Firth of Forth in the shadow of the world famous Forth Bridge (a stunning piece of Victorian engineering) and the more recent Forth Bridge Road. The historic cobbled High Street is replete with bars and quality restaurants, while on the town's fringes are the three grand country houses of Dundas, Dalmeny (➤ 143) and **Hopetoun House,** the latter two open to the public. Waterfront strolls, the **Queensferry Museum** and a scenic bus or train ride out to the royal burgh make an ideal day trip.

➕ *Greater City inset map 7a* ✉ South Queensferry 🚌 First Bus 43 or Stagecoach Fife 747, 53, 55, X50, followed by a walk

Hopetoun House

✉ By South Queensferry ☎ 0131 331 2451; www.hopetoun.co.uk 🕓 Easter weekend to last weekend in September daily 10:30–5 (last admissions 4pm) 🚌 First Bus 43

Queensferry Museum

✉ 53 High Street ☎ 0131 331 5545 🕓 Mon, Thu–Sat 10–1, 2:15–5 ✋ Free 🚌 First Bus 43

HOTELS

GLASGOW
Blythswood Square (£££)
Opened late in 2009, this new luxury contender aims to be a match for Hotel du Vin. With a more central location, luxurious rooms, a health spa and private screening room it is already realising its dream. It's owned by the same people behind the Howard and the Bonham in Edinburgh.

✉ Blythswood Square ☎ 0141 208 2458; www.blythswoodsquare.com

Brunswick Hotel (££)
A modern stylish hotel in a building that offers plenty of architectural interest. Completed in 1995, it offers good-value accommodation and high-quality service, together with an excellent cafe.

✉ 106–108 Brunswick Street ☎ 0141 552 0001; www.brunswickhotel.co.uk
🚉 Queen Street (5-min walk), Central Station (10-min walk)

Hotel du Vin (£££)
Now under the Hotel du Vin brand, arguably Glasgow's finest hotel just keeps on getting better and better. Neat touches include golf putters and putting machines in many rooms; the lavish public areas also impress. The hotel's restaurant is first-rate too.

✉ 1 Devonshire Gardens ☎ 0141 399 2001; www.hotelduvin.com/glasgow

PEEBLES
Castle Venlaw Hotel (£££)
This cosy, 12-bedroom, family-run hotel stands in forested hillside overlooking Peebles. Of the revamped rooms the Honeymoon Suite is the highlight with its four-poster and champagne cooler in the bathroom. Excellent restaurant too.

✉ Edinburgh Road ☎ 01721 720384; www.venlaw.co.uk

ROSLIN
Roslin Glen Hotel (££)
Comfortable and friendly hotel 11km (7 miles) south of Edinburgh,

well placed for Rosslyn Chapel (➤ 174–175) and Roslin Castle,
with personal service and a good restaurant.
✉ 2 Penicuik Road ☎ 0131 440 2029

RESTAURANTS

GLASGOW

City Merchant (£££)

Family-run central restaurant since 1988, specializing in Scottish
produce. The menu offers a selection of superb fish and seafood,
beef and lamb dishes and vegetarian options, using only the
freshest and most high quality ingredients.
✉ 97–99 Candleriggs ☎ 0141 553 1577; www.citymerchant.co.uk
🕔 Mon–Sat 12–10:30

Fratelli Sarti (££)

A great 100 per cent Italian, family-run restaurant and bistro.
There is also a deli on the side. Expect authentic, down-to-earth
cucina casalinga at good prices. Very busy at weekends. There
are two further branches in the city, in Renfield Street and
Wellington Street.
✉ 121 Bath Street ☎ 0141 204 0440; www.sarti.co.uk 🕔 Mon–Fri 8–10:30,
Sat 10–10:30, Sun 12–10:30

Gamba (££)

Superb cuisine at this popular and award-winning restaurant
specializing in fish, shellfish and seafood. Steaks and vegetarian
dishes are always available and there are good value pre- and post-
theatre menus on offer.
✉ 225a West George Street ☎ 0141 572 0899; www.gamba.co.uk
🕔 Mon–Sat 12–2:30, 5–10:30

Mother India (££)

This is part of a rapidly expanding empire that now includes a
restaurant in Edinburgh. Mother India is set across three floors and
is more fine dining than Indian takeaway. In a city overflowing with
excellent Indian restaurants, this is arguably the best place to try
Indian food in the UK outside London. Fresh ingredients and

cooking to order are the key, not to mention ice-cold Indian beers and smooth service.

✉ 28 Westminster Terrace ☎ 0141 221 1663; www.motherindiaglasgow.co.uk 🕐 Mon–Thu 12–10, Fri–Sat 12–11, Sun 12–10

Two Fat Ladies at The Buttery (£££)

There are two branches of this acclaimed restaurant, the original in Dumbarton Road and this one (opened in 2008 in Argyle Street in the city centre) which is more contemporary and plusher than its sister. This is *the* place for fish and seafood lovers as it uses the best local catches.

✉ 652 Argyle Street ☎ 0141 221 8188 🕐 Mon–Sat 12–3, 5–10:30 (Fri, Sat until 11), Sun 1:30–9:30

The Ubiquitous Chip (£££)

A Glasgow institution, this established West End restaurant has been serving the best of Scottish cuisine in stylish surroundings since 1971. Enjoy traditional but imaginative dishes, with plenty of game and venison dishes on offer.

✉ 12 Ashton Lane, Hillhead ☎ 0141 334 5007; www.ubiquitouschip.co.uk 🕐 Mon–Sat 12–2:30, 5:30–11, Sun 12:30–2:30, 6:30–1

HADDINGTON

Waterside (£)

This popular award-winning restaurant and bistro is attractively sited beside the River Tyne, with an outside terrace area from which to enjoy the splendid views of the historic St Mary's Church. It offers fine bar luncheons and suppers, as well as more substantial restaurant meals.

✉ 1–5 Waterside, Nungate ☎ 01620 825674 🕐 Daily 12–2, 6–10

LINLITHGOW

Champany Inn (£££)

Perhaps the best steaks in Scotland are on offer at this remarkable restaurant that recently won its first Michelin star. It is not cheap, but the journey out to West Lothian is worth it for the 28-day hung beef cooked perfectly on a chargrill. The lobster tank and world-class wine list round off an experience up there with anything in Edinburgh itself.

✉ Champany Farm House ☎ 01506 834 532; www.champany.com
🕐 Mon–Fri lunch 12:30–2, dinner 7–10; Sat dinner only 7–10

The Four Marys (£)

Friendly pub and restaurant themed on the serving-women of the ill-fated Mary, Queen of Scots, with excellent lunches and evening meals served daily, and a wide range of real ales

✉ 65 High Street ☎ 01506 842171; www.thefourmarys.co.uk 🕐 Mon–Fri 12–3, 5–9; Sat–Sun 12:30–9

Livingston's (££–£££)

Tucked away at the end of a lane, Livingston's is the place to go for an authentic Scottish experience. Ruby red fabrics, tartan carpets and soft candlelight create a relaxed atmosphere that enhances the menu featuring local ingredients such as Inverurie lamb, Highland venison and Stornoway black pudding.

✉ 52 High Street ☎ 01506 846565; www.livingstons-restaurant.co.uk
🕐 Tue–Sat 12–2:30, 6–9:30

SOUTH QUEENSFERRY

Orocco Pier (££)

You get spectacular views of the Forth bridges and contemporary cuisine in this slick oasis in the waterfront suburb of South Queensferry. Seafood features prominently on the menu.

✉ 17 The High Street ☎ 0870 118 1664; www.oroccopier.co.uk 🕐 Daily
8am–10pm 🚌 43

SHOPPING

GLASGOW

The Barras

A large covered and open market that has become an institution, with more than 1,000 traders selling every imaginable item.

✉ 244 Gallowgate ☎ 0141 552 4601; www.glasgow-barrowland.com
🕐 Sat–Sun 10–5

Italian Centre

This groups of shops stocks the best of all things Italian, particularly fashion items, in a stylish mall.

✉ 7 John Street ☎ 0141 552 6368

St Enoch Centre

One of the largest glass-roofed constructions in Europe houses a wide range of high-street stores, as well as independent retailers and places to eat. There is a car park and an ice rink at this recently revamped mall.

✉ 55 St Enoch Square ☎ 0141 204 3900; www.st-enoch.co.uk

LIVINGSTON
Livingston Designer Outlet

This huge outlet offers excellent discounts on designer clothes. A cinema complex, bars, cafes and restaurants make this an ideal place to visit for a rainy day. The new Elements Square development opened next door in 2009, providing a further array of stores and eating venues.

✉ Almondvale Avenue ☎ 01505 423961; www.shopthecentre.co.uk

CHILDREN'S ATTRACTIONS

FALKIRK
The Falkirk Wheel

This marvel of modern engineering, the only rotating boat lift in the world, reconnects the Glasgow to Edinburgh canal system and will impress all ages. The visitor centre explains it all and there is an excellent children's play area, gift shop and cafe. Boat trips daily all year.

✉ Lime Road, Tamfourhill ☎ 08700 500 208; www.thefalkirkwheel.co.uk
🎫 Visitor centre: free. Boat trip: expensive

LIVINGSTON
Almond Valley Heritage Trust

Innovative museum of the history of West Lothian, whose narrow-gauge railway, farmyard animals, play areas and games provide an interesting day out for all the family. In a pleasant riverside setting.

✉ Millfield ☎ 01506 414957; www.almondvalley.co.uk 🕓 Daily 10–5
✋ Moderate

NORTH QUEENSFERRY
Deep-Sea World

Scotland's national aquarium at North Queensferry provides education and great entertainment in a purpose-designed environment. The highlight is the shark tunnel (reputed to be the largest in the world), which takes you on a moving walkway right into the world of giant sharks

✉ North Queensferry ☎ 01383 411880; www.deepseaworld.com
🕓 Mon–Fri 10–5, Sat–Sun 10–6 ✋ Moderate

SPORT AND ACTIVITIES

CRUISE
Maid of the Forth

Take a 3-hour evening cruise on the Firth of Forth, with a heated saloon, bar and a resident jazz band. Spectacular views of seals and the bridges (➤ 28 for day cruises). Optional barbecue.

✉ Hawes Pier, South Queensferry ☎ 0131 331 5000;
www.maidoftheforth.co.uk 🚌 43

GUIDED TOURS
Glenkinchie Distellery Visitor Centre

This facility, 24km (15 miles) southeast of Edinburgh, offers a rare chance to witness the distilling process in the south of Scotland, with a guided tour showing how the whisky is made.

✉ Glenkinchie Distillery, Pencaitland, Tranent ☎ 01875 340333
🕓 Easter–Nov daily; Dec–Easter Mon–Fri

SAILING
Port Edgar Sailing School

The largest watersport centre in Scotland, on the Firth of Forth, close to the bridges, with tuition and boat rental for dinghy and catamaran sailing, canoeing and powerboating.

✉ Shore Road, South Queensferry ☎ 0131 331 3330;
www.edinburghleisure.co.uk 🚌 First Bus 43

Index

Street Index

Acknowledgements

The Automobile Association would like to thank the following photographers, companies and picture libraries for their assistance in the preparation of this book.

Abbreviations for the picture credits are as follows – (t) top; (b) bottom; (c) centre; (l) left; (r) right; (AA) AA World Travel Library.

4l Arthur's Seat, AA/K Paterson; **4c** Taxi, Edinburgh Inspiring Capital; **4r** Edinburgh Castle, AA/R Elliott; **5l** Snowsport Centre, Edinburgh Inspiring Capital; **5c** Victoria Street, Edinburgh Inspiring Capital; **5r** Linlithgow Palace, AA/K Paterson; **6/7** Arthur's Seat, AA/K Paterson; **8/9** Military tattoo, AA/J Smith; **10tr** Fireworks, Edinburgh Inspiring Capital; **10cr** Pipe Band, Edinburgh Inspiring Capital; **10br** Whisky, AA/A Baker; **11tl** Water of Leith, AA/D Corrance; **11tr** Princes Street, AA/K Paterson; **11br** Edinburgh Close, Edinburgh Inspiring Capital; **12/13t** Seafood, AA/E Ellington; **12/13c** Haggis, AA/J Henderson; **12br** Oysters, AA/C Sawyer; **13tr** Roast beef, AA/C Sawyer; **13cr** Kippers, AA/R Coulam; **13hr** Haggis, AA/J Ourrie, **14/15** Whisky, AA/J Smith; **14br** Shortbread, AA/J Freeman; **15t** Oatmeal, Photodisc; **15cr** Pheasant, AA/J Smith; **15bl** Raspberry elina, AA/J Freeman; **15br** Shortbread, AA/K Paterson; **16c** Bus, AA/K Paterson; **16bl** Victoria Street, AA/S Whitehorne; **16/17** View over Edinburgh, AA/D Corrance; **17** Balloon Man, Edinburgh Inspiring Capital; **18** Scott Monument, AA/J Smith; **18/19** Whisky, AA/J Smith; **19tr** Georgian facade, Edinburgh Inspiring Capital; **19cr** Princes Street gardens, AA/K Paterson; **20/21** Taxi, Edinburgh Inspiring Capital; **26** Waverley Station, Edinburgh Inspiring Capital; **28** Taxi, Edinburgh Inspiring Capital; **30/31** Postbox, Edinburgh Inspiring Capital; **34/35** View from Calton Hill, AA/R Elliott; **36/37** Arthur's Seat, AA/K Blackwell; **38** Edinburgh Castle, AA/J Beazley; **38/39** Fireworks, AA; **39** Robert the Bruce, AA/J Smith; **40/41** Museum of Scotland, AA/K Paterson; **41** Museum of Scotland interior, Edinburgh Inspiring Capital; **42** Busts, AA/K Paterson; **43tl** National Gallery of Scotland, AA/K Paterson; **43br** National Gallery of Scotland exterior, Edinburgh Inspiring Capital; **44** New Town door, AA/J Smith; **45** New Town, Edinburgh Inspiring Capital; **46** Our Dynamic Earth detail, Edinburgh Inspiring Capital; **46/47** Our Dynamic Earth, Edinburgh Inspiring Capital; **48** Lantern, AA/D Corrance; **48/49t** Gate detail, AA/J Smith; **48/49b** Palace of Holyroodhouse, AA/J Smith; **50** Entrance gate, AA/J Love; **50/51** Lily pond, AA/K Paterson; **51** Sign, AA/J Love; **52** Gladstone's Land, AA/J Smith; **52/53** Back of Royal Mile, AA/J Smith; **53** Deacon Brodies' Tavern, AA/J Smith; **54** Walter Scott, AA/S Whitehorne; **55** Scott Monument, Edinburgh Inspiring Capital; **56/57** Snowsport Centre, Edinburgh Inspiring Capital; **58/59** Grassmarket, Edinburgh Inspiring Capital; **60/61** Tartan, AA/S Whitehorne; **62** Child with kid, AA/E Davies; **64** City Chambers, AA/K Paterson; **64/65** Royal Mile, AA/K Paterson; **65tl** St Giles' Cathedral, AA/K Blackwell; **65cr** Abbey Strand, AA/K Paterson; **66/67** The Meadows, Edinburgh Inspiring Capital; **68/69** Edinburgh skyline, Edinburgh Inspiring Capital; **70/71** Sherlock Holmes, AA/J Love; **72/73** Pub, AA/J Smith; **74/75** Victoria Street, Edinburgh Inspiring Capital; **77** The Hub, AA/J Smith; **78** Camera Obscura, AA/K Paterson; **79** Camera Obscura sign, AA/K Paterson; **80/81** Edinburgh Exchange, AA/J Smith; **82/83** The Hub, AA/K Paterson; **83** Gladstone's Land, AA/K Paterson; **84/85** Grassmarket, Edinburgh Inspiring Capital; **86/87** The Meadows, Edinburgh Inspiring Capital; **88/89b** Parliament Square, AA/K Paterson; **89t** West Parliament Square, AA/K Paterson; **90/91** Stained glass window, AA/J Smith; **91tr** St Giles cathedral, AA/J Smith; **91bl** Scotch Whisky Heritage Centre, AA/K Paterson; **92** Victoria Street, AA/J Smith; **93** Victoria Street, AA/K Paterson; **101** Holyrood Park, AA/K Paterson; **102** Holyrood Abbey, AA/K Paterson; **104tl** John Knox's House, AA/J Smith; **104/105** John Knox's House, AA/K Paterson; **105tr** Museum of Childhood, AA/K Paterson; **106** Model in regimental dress, AA/K Paterson; **107** The People's Story, AA/K Paterson; **108/109** Scottish Parliament, Adam Elder/Scottish Parliament; **113** Skyline, Edinburgh Inspiring Capital; **115** Calton Hill, Edinburgh Inspiring Capital; **116** New Town, AA/J Smith; **116/117** Charlotte Square, AA/J Smith; **118/119** The Georgian House, AA/K Paterson; **119cr** The Mound, AA/K Paterson; **120/121** Princes Street, AA/J Smith; **122** Ross fountain, AA/J Smith; **122/123** Royal Scottish Academy, AA/K Paterson; **124cl** Home of Robert Louis Stevenson, AA/K Paterson; **124/125** New Town, Edinburgh Inspiring Capital; **125tl** Scott Monument, AA/J Smith; **125br** Princes Street Gardens, AA/J Smith; **126/127** Scottish National Portrait Gallery, AA/K Paterson; **139** Water of Leith, Edinburgh Inspiring Capital; **140/141** View from Braid Hills, AA/K Paterson; **141bl** The Colonies, AA/K Paterson; **142/143** Craigmillar Castle, AA; **143bl** Cramond, AA/K Paterson; **144** Dean village, AA/K Paterson; **145** Duddingston, Edinburgh Inspiring Capital; **146/147** Edinburgh Zoo, AA/D Corrance; **147br** Leith, AA/K Paterson; **148cl** Murrayfield Stadium, AA/K Paterson; **148/149** Royal Scottish Observatory, AA/K Paterson; **150** Royal Yacht Britannia, AA/K Paterson; **152tl** Stockbridge, Edinburgh Inspiring Capital; **152/153** Swanston, AA/D Corrance; **154tr** St Bernard's Well, AA; **154bl** Stockbridge, AA/K Paterson; **155** Dean Village, AA/K Paterson; **162/163** Linlithgow Palace, AA/K Paterson; **165** The Burrell Collection, AA/S Whitehorne; **166** House for an Art Lover, AA/S Whitehorne; **168/169** Linlithgow Palace, AA/K Paterson; **170** Concorde in the Museum of Flight, AA/K Blackwell; **171br** Tantallon Castle, AA/K Paterson; **172/173** Neidpath Castle, AA/M Taylor; **174/175** Rosslyn Chapel, AA/R Elliott.

Every effort has been made to trace the copyright holders, and we apologise in advance for any accidental errors. We would be happy to apply the corrections in the following edition of this publication.

Sight Locator Index

This index relates to the maps on the cover. We have given map references to the main sights in the book. Some sights may not be plotted on the maps.

Dear Reader

Your comments, opinions and recommendations are very important to us. Please help us to improve our travel guides by taking a few minutes to complete this simple questionnaire.

You do not need a stamp (unless posted outside the UK). If you do not want to cut this page from your guide, then photocopy it or write your answers on a plain sheet of paper.

Send to: **The Editor, AA World Travel Guides,**
FREEPOST SCE 4598, Basingstoke RG21 4GY.

Your recommendations...

We always encourage readers' recommendations for restaurants, nightlife or shopping – if your recommendation is used in the next edition of the guide, we will send you a **FREE AA Guide** of your choice from this series. Please state below the establishment name, location and your reasons for recommending it.

_____

_____

_____

_____

_____

Please send me **AA Guide** _____

About this guide...

Which title did you buy?

AA _____

Where did you buy it? _____

When? <u>m m</u> / <u>y y</u>

Why did you choose this guide? _____

_____

_____

_____

_____

Did this guide meet your expectations?

Exceeded ☐ Met all ☐ Met most ☐ Fell below ☐

Were there any aspects of this guide that you particularly liked? _____

_____

_____

_____

continued on next page...

Is there anything we could have done better? _____

_____

_____

_____

_____

About you...

Name (Mr/Mrs/Ms) _____

Address _____

_____

_____ Postcode _____

Daytime tel nos _____

Email _____

Please only give us your mobile phone number or email if you wish to hear from us about other products and services from the AA and partners by text or rmms, or email.

Which age group are you in?

Under 25 ☐ 25–34 ☐ 35–44 ☐ 45–54 ☐ 55–64 ☐ 65+ ☐

How many trips do you make a year?

Less than one ☐ One ☐ Two ☐ Three or more ☐

Are you an AA member? Yes ☐ No ☐

About your trip...

When did you book? mm/yy When did you travel? mm/yy

How long did you stay? _____

Was it for business or leisure? _____

Did you buy any other travel guides for your trip? _____

If yes, which ones? _____

_____

_____

_____

Thank you for taking the time to complete this questionnaire. Please send it to us as soon as possible, and remember, you do not need a stamp (unless posted outside the UK).

AA Travel Insurance call 0800 072 4168 or visit www.theAA.com